Contents

KU-495-660

We deliberately haven't put any _essay_ answers in this book, because they'd just be repeating what's in the revision guide. Instead, we've put in a section about how to write good essay answers, and do well. Answers for the _numerical_ questions are included though, on page 108.

How Businesses Work

Businesses are like celebrities. They get everywhere and they do pretty much anything you care to mention.
These pages are for AQA, OCR, Edexcel and WJEC.

Most **Businesses** exist to make a **Profit**

1) Businesses aim to make a profit by selling **products** (physical **objects** — also called **goods**) or **services** (things that **can't** be picked up and touched), e.g. a car manufacturer sells a product, and a hair salon sells a service.

2) Some firms sell **necessities** — products or services that people **need** (such as gas, electricity, clothes and food). Other firms sell **luxury** products and services — that people **want** but don't need (like holidays and jewellery).

3) Businesses have to **make a profit** or **break even** to survive.

4) This is especially true in the **private sector** — if a business doesn't make enough money to survive it could go **bankrupt** and have to **close down**.

public sector = government-owned
private sector = privately owned

5) In the **public sector**, things aren't as clear-cut. Organisations like the army, the police, hospitals and state schools aren't there to **make money** — they provide a service to the community. **Charities** are another exception. For more on not-for-profit businesses, see p. 15.

As well as making a profit, businesses may have **other objectives**, such as:

- Offering the **highest quality** goods and services possible.
- Increasing their **market share**.
- Giving good **customer service**.
- Having a good **image** and **reputation**.
- Trying to limit their **impact** on the **environment**.

Market share is how much of the market a firm has compared to its competitors.

Businesses might **give up some profit** to help them meet **other objectives**, but most business owners are **ultimately** only interested in **profit**. Everything else comes **after**.

Businesses all need certain **Key Things**

Before businesses can sell stuff and make a profit, they need certain things:

There's more on different sources of finance on p. 18-19.

1)	**Labour**	Businesses need people to do the work.
2)	**Finance**	It costs money to provide goods and services.
3)	**Customers**	Every business needs people to buy the goods and services, and pay for them.
4)	**Suppliers**	Suppliers provide raw materials, equipment and human resources.
5)	**Premises**	Businesses need buildings to work in.
6)	**Enterprise**	Entrepreneurs come up with original ideas and take risks to make a profit.

Businesses have several different **Functions**

Production of products or services isn't enough on its own — businesses have **other tasks** to do before they can **make a profit**. These different tasks are usually looked after by different departments.

Business departments and their roles

Production	A business turns **raw materials** into a finished **good** or **service** that they can sell. They must also monitor the **quality** of what they are producing.
Finance	Businesses have to keep a careful eye on their finances. They must keep detailed and accurate **financial records**. A business must try to get the best **value for money** for every pound it spends.
HRM	(**Human Resources Management**) Businesses must make sure they have the right number of employees of the right quality in the right place at the right time.
Marketing	Businesses have to identify what customers **want** or **need** and figure out how best to **sell** it to them.
Admin	Businesses have to **run their own affairs** as efficiently as possible.
R&D	(**Research and Development**) Businesses may need to discover **new ideas** for products that might be wanted in the future, and get them ready to be launched onto the market.

1) Businesses need to **plan** what activities to do in the future.

2) They need to **control** what their employees are doing, and control the amount of money that's spent.

3) Businesses need to **coordinate** all their different functions and departments and make sure that all the departments are working towards common objectives.

AS-Level
Business
Studies

The Revision Guide

Editors:

Rachael Powers, Jennifer Underwood, Emma Warhurst

Contributors:

Angela Anthonisz, Paul Brockbank, Charley Darbishire, Peter Gray, Gemma Hallam,
Jeff Harris, Jane Hosking, Rebecca May, David Morris, Adrian Murray, Andy Park,
Kate Redmond, Katherine Reed, Julie Watkins, Keith Williamson

Proofreaders:

Eleanor Ellington, Glenn Rogers and Victoria Skelton

Published by Coordination Group Publications Ltd.

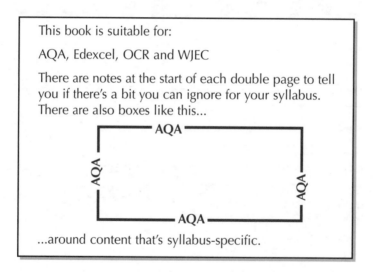

This book is suitable for:

AQA, Edexcel, OCR and WJEC

There are notes at the start of each double page to tell
you if there's a bit you can ignore for your syllabus.
There are also boxes like this...

AQA
AQA   AQA
AQA

...around content that's syllabus-specific.

ISBN: 978 1 84762 133 7

Groovy website: www.cgpbooks.co.uk
Jolly bits of clipart from CorelDRAW®
Printed by Elanders Hindson Ltd, Newcastle upon Tyne.

Based on the classic CGP style created by Richard Parsons.

How Businesses Work

Businesses *also have to meet the* Needs *of* Stakeholders

Everyone who is affected by a business is called a **stakeholder**. There are two types: **internal** and **external** stakeholders.

INTERNAL STAKEHOLDERS — People inside the business

1) The **owners** are the most important stakeholders. They make a profit if the business is successful and decide what happens to the business. In a limited company, the **shareholders** are the owners.

2) **Employees** are interested in their **job security** and **promotion** prospects. They also want to earn a **decent wage** and have **pleasant working conditions**. **Managers** have **extra concerns** — they'll probably get some of the blame if the company does badly, and some of the credit if things go well.

EXTERNAL STAKEHOLDERS — People outside the business

1) **Customers** want **high quality** products and services at **low prices**.

2) **Suppliers** are the people and businesses who sell **raw materials** to the business. The business provides them with their **income** — if it can't pay quickly enough, the suppliers can have **cash flow** problems.

3) Most businesses are run on **credit**. **Creditors** (people who are owed money by the business, such as suppliers) have a stake in the business. They want to make sure they get paid on time.

4) The **local community** will **gain** if the business provides **local employment** and **sponsors** local activities. The community will **suffer** if the business causes noise and pollution, or if the business has to **cut jobs**.

5) The **government** gets more in **taxes** when the business makes good profits.

A business is **accountable** to its stakeholders. It has to satisfy their needs and answer their criticisms. However, some stakeholders are **more important** to the business than others.

1) A business can't ignore its **customers**. If the business **can't sell** its products, it'll go **bust**.

2) No limited company can afford to ignore its **shareholders**. If they're unhappy with the way things are run, they can **sack the directors** or **sell** the business to **someone else**.

— WJEC, OCR and Edexcel —

There are Advantages *to owning a business*

1) Individuals who start up their own companies are called **entrepreneurs**. There's more about them on p.6-7.

2) People usually only set up their own business if they expect to make **more** than they could earn working as an **employee** of another company.

3) People may set up their own business so that they can be **their own boss** and make their own decisions — so they don't have to answer to anyone else.

4) Setting up your own business can also give you the opportunity to do a job you're really **interested** in.

Practice Questions

Q1 What objectives might a private sector business have? Which objective is the most important and why?

Q2 Name at least four essential things that a business needs to produce goods and services.

Q3 Explain what the term 'stakeholder' means.

Q4 Give three benefits of owning your own business.

Exam Questions

Q1 To what extent do businesses only exist to make a profit? (10 marks)

Q2 Discuss the different types of stakeholder in a large company, and explain their importance to the company. (6 marks)

But does the steak holder come with a chips holder...

This first section covers fairly basic business ideas. If you've done GCSE Business Studies, some of it might seem a bit dull. Don't assume you already know it all though — it's worth reading through to make sure you really know what's what. Some of these things will crop up again later in the book — so stick with this section. And then go on to the good stuff...

WJEC, OCR and Edexcel

What Businesses Do

Never mind what businesses do — what would you do without business? (Well, you'd spend less time revising this, for a start). Anyway...businesses transform raw materials into finished products, and try to make a profit. **For all four boards.**

Businesses **Add Value** to raw materials

1) Businesses **pay** for raw materials, then **transform** them into finished products and **sell** them. Customers pay more for the finished product than the business originally paid for the raw materials used to make it.

2) The difference between the **cost** of the raw materials bought by the business to make each product and the **price** the customer pays for the finished product is known as the **value added**.
E.g. if a bakery buys the ingredients for a cake for **80p** and sells the finished cake for **£3**, the value added is £3 – £0.80 = **£2.20**.

3) The value added leaves a **surplus** — the business uses that to pay its other costs (e.g. wages, rent and electricity — see p. 30 for more on costs), and any money left over is **profit**.

4) Some products have **high** value added — usually **luxury** items like designer clothes or meals in expensive restaurants. Other products, like basic groceries, have much **lower** value added.

5) The greater the **value added**, the higher the **profits** are likely to be — businesses want the value added to be as high as possible in order to increase their profits.

Betty had plenty of raw materials — now all she needed to do was work out how to add value.

The **Supply Chain** is the product's journey from **Raw Materials** to **Consumer**

1) Raw materials go through various stages on their way to reaching the consumer as a finished product. These stages all form part of the **supply chain**.

2) The supply chain always starts with **raw materials** and finishes with the **consumer**, and the intermediate stages usually include suppliers, manufacturing, distribution (getting products into shops so that customers can buy them) and retailers.

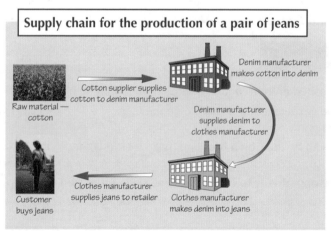

Supply chain for the production of a pair of jeans

Raw material — cotton

Cotton supplier supplies cotton to denim manufacturer

Denim manufacturer makes cotton into denim

Denim manufacturer supplies denim to clothes manufacturer

Clothes manufacturer makes denim into jeans

Clothes manufacturer supplies jeans to retailer

Customer buys jeans

3) The various steps in the supply chain often happen in different businesses and different places.

4) All businesses — wherever they are in the supply chain — are dependent on their **suppliers** and **customers** — e.g. a problem with cocoa bean crops in Africa may cause a problem for a shop selling chocolate bars in England.

5) **Value** is normally added at **each stage** in the supply chain — e.g. a bead-making factory turns plastic into beads, which can be sold for more than the plastic was worth. If a handbag manufacturer uses the beads to decorate handbags, the finished handbags will be sold for more than it cost the manufacturer to buy the fabric and beads.

Businesses have to make **Compromises**

1) Businesses have a **limited** amount of **money** and other **resources**, so they try to make the most of the resources available to them in order to maximise **profits**. However, they **can't** usually do **everything** that they might want to achieve.

2) Businesses make decisions that they expect will result in **profits**, but there is always a **cost** involved in every decision they make. E.g. if a business decides to spend £15 000 on changing its brand logo, it can't spend that £15 000 again, so there is an **opportunity cost** involved — it could have spent the money on an advertising campaign that might have generated an extra £50 000 of revenue (see p. 31 for more on opportunity cost).

3) Businesses also have to make **trade-offs** — they have to **sacrifice** one thing in order to **gain** another. E.g. a restaurant might want to charge low prices to its customers, but this might mean that they have to use low quality ingredients — sacrificing quality for value. Or a furniture company might produce sofas and chairs that are good for the spine, but not very attractive — sacrificing aesthetics for function.

What Businesses Do

Businesses can be classified by Production Stage — AQA, WJEC and OCR

You can classify businesses according to the **stage** of the **production process** (from raw material to finished product) that the business is involved in. There are three divisions — **primary**, **secondary** and **tertiary**.

Primary Sector

1) The primary sector **extracts raw materials** from natural resources. It includes **farming**, **fishing** and **mining**.

2) Primary sector industries are in **decline** in the UK, mainly because it is often **cheaper** to **import** raw materials from other countries, and trade barriers have made it more **difficult** for UK companies to **export** raw materials. E.g. in 1984 there were **170** coal mines open around the UK — more than **150** of these have now been **closed**.

3) There has also been a decline in the number of people employed in **farming** — the number of people working in farming in the UK is now **less than half** what it was at the start of the 1970s.

Secondary Sector

1) The secondary sector **processes** the raw materials that come from the primary sector.

2) Secondary industry includes **manufacturing** (e.g. cars, tinned food, steel) and **construction** (e.g. building houses, factories, roads).

3) Secondary sector industries have also been **declining** in the UK for the past 25 years, mainly because companies are **moving** production to other parts of the world where manufacturing costs are **lower**. This increases their profits, because they can produce their products more cheaply, but still sell their products to UK consumers at the same price. E.g. in 2006, **645** jobs were lost at Nestlé's chocolate factory in York when Nestlé moved production of several products to Europe.

Tertiary Sector

1) This is the **service sector** which provides services (like banking) to individuals and to **businesses** in the primary and secondary sectors.

2) Examples include shops, banks, insurance companies, restaurants, hotels, and healthcare services.

3) In most developed countries the tertiary sector has **expanded** over the last few decades — the UK economy is now mainly made up of tertiary sector companies.

4) The main tertiary sector growth in the UK has been in **financial** and **business** services like banking and accounting — the proportion of people working in these jobs in the UK has **doubled** in the last 25 years.

Jon was glad to hear that the tertiary sector was on the increase — he'd always wanted to be an accountant.

Practice Questions

Q1 Give two examples of products with high value added.

Q2 What is the supply chain?

Q3 Give an example of: a) a primary sector business, b) a secondary sector business, c) a tertiary sector business.

Q4 Which is the main production sector in the UK?

Exam Question

Q1 Prawn Free sell salmon fishcakes. Analyse how a drop in salmon supplies might affect their supply chain. (10 marks)

I'm in the middle of a (supply) chain reaction...

The whole point of businesses is to add value to whatever they buy so that they can sell it for more than they paid for it — simple really. Learn the definitions of primary, secondary and tertiary sector businesses and a couple of examples of each in case you're asked for them in the exam. And don't forget about the supply chain — it affects all businesses.

Enterprise and Entrepreneurs

Starting a small business is easy, but making a living out of it is hard — it's not just about having an idea.
These pages are for AQA, Edexcel and WJEC, but they might be useful for OCR students too.

People who start businesses are called Entrepreneurs

1) An entrepreneur is a person (or one of a group of people) who **raises the resources** and **organises the activities** needed to **start a business**.

2) Once an entrepreneur has an **idea** for a new business, they have to organise everything they need to set up the business, including financial investment, staff, buildings, research and development, and marketing.

3) If the entrepreneur **organises** things well, and consumers **want** the good or service, the business will succeed. If they get it **wrong** the business will have to give up and stop trading.

> EXAMPLE: **Richard Branson** was only 20 when he set up **Virgin** as a mail-order music retailer. He then continued to **expand** the company to include a record shop and recording studio, and it now includes air travel, mobile, internet, rail and music services. Richard Branson is one of the **wealthiest** men in Britain, and he was **knighted** for services to business in 1999.

Entrepreneurs are Innovative Risk-takers, Planners and Organisers

1) Successful entrepreneurs tend to be **creative** — they're **innovators** who have spotted a **gap in the market**. A gap in the market is either an **original idea**, or a way of making an **existing** idea **different** from the competition, e.g. selling goods to a new segment of the market.

2) They **work hard** and have **perseverance** and **resilience**. James Dyson took 20 years to get his design of vacuum cleaner to the market because he couldn't get an existing manufacturer to adopt his ideas. Finally, he raised the **finance** himself and started his **own small firm** to make what's now one of the best-selling cleaners in the world.

3) They're **risk-takers**. When starting a business, many entrepreneurs have to have the **confidence** to use their **own financial resources** to provide start-up capital. If the business fails, they lose their investment. They're **prepared** to take the risk because they believe that they will gain financial **rewards** — they're motivated by **profit**.

4) They're **planners**. Successful entrepreneurs plan what financial, technical and human resources they'll need.

5) They're **good organisers** and organise resources so that they're used cost-effectively.

Entrepreneurs research Profitable Business Opportunities

Entrepreneurs get ideas for new businesses from **brainstorming** or from personal or professional **experience**.

1) They need to consider the strengths and weaknesses of each idea. E.g. there might be lots of demand for a new Italian restaurant, but no suitable premises to locate the business in.

2) Successful entrepreneurs won't **commit** large resources to an idea until they feel confident that it will **work**. They need to know that there's enough **demand** for their product or service and that they have the **skills** to produce it.

3) Entrepreneurs need to work out how much money they'll make — it's only worth going ahead with a business idea if it's **profitable**. If they're not likely to make big profits then it's not worth the **risk**.

4) A new business won't usually attract customers unless it can offer something different — a **unique selling point**. This could be quality, low price, good customer service etc.

5) It's really important to get the **price** right. If the price is too high, sales will be too low to make enough money. If the price is too low, the total revenue won't be enough.

The Government encourages Enterprise

1) The UK government encourages entrepreneurs to start their own businesses because enterprise benefits the **economy** — new businesses **increase productivity** and create **new jobs**. The government is particularly keen to promote enterprise in areas that need **economic regeneration**.

2) The government has set up organisations like **Business Link** to provide **advice** and **support** to owners of small businesses and to people thinking of starting their own business. They can offer advice on many aspects of setting up and running a small business, including creating a business plan and financing a new business.

3) The government also provides **grants** and **incentives** for entrepreneurs to set up businesses. Entrepreneurs can get grants from various sources, including local authorities and **Regional Development Agencies** like Yorkshire Forward and Advantage West Midlands (see p. 17 for more on this). The **Enterprise Investment Scheme** is another government scheme that offers tax incentives to people who invest in small businesses.

Enterprise and Entrepreneurs

Entrepreneurs have to do *Market Research* on a *Small Budget*

1) Before start-up, it's important to get to know the **market**. Entrepreneurs need to know about social, environmental, legal and economic factors that can limit how they market their product.

2) New businesses can easily do **secondary research** (looking at data that's already available) on a **small budget**, and they can also do low-budget **primary market research** (gathering new data) — this may be a **survey** asking potential customers their opinions of an idea, or **observation** of activities in a similar business.

3) It's really important to be **objective** and **scientific** when doing your own primary research. It's easy and tempting to ask **loaded questions** that lead people into giving the answer you want. It's easy to ask **friends** and **family** who give "nice" answers out of politeness. Watch out for this in exam questions — the new business owner in the case study may have done **unreliable** market research. You'd be spot-on to **question** their methods and their findings. For more on market research, see p. 82-83.

Entrepreneurs have to do *Marketing* on a *Budget* too

1) At the start, a new business doesn't have loads of money to spend on **advertising** campaigns. An advert in the **local paper** and a few **leaflets** are probably going to be the limit.

2) **Sales promotions** can be **cheap** to organise. Special offers like "buy one, get one free" tend to get people buying.

3) It's important to not stimulate demand **too much** — when demand is greater than the **capacity** of the business, the business has to turn customers away, which isn't good for customer relations, and can cause the business to fail. For more on marketing, see p. 78-79.

New businesses often *Fail*

New start-ups are risky — lots of small businesses **fail** within a couple of years of starting up. The reasons for this vary from business to business, but it's often because:

> Nearly all new businesses have limited resources so they have to be very careful about what they spend when they're setting up.

1) Some entrepreneurs lack **experience**. Small business owners, especially **sole traders** (see p.12), have to be a "Jack of all trades" — they're responsible for running all aspects of the business, including finance, managing employees, marketing, etc. Many entrepreneurs don't have enough experience to do all these things properly.

2) Entrepreneurs may have false **expectations** of what running their own business will be like — they expect huge profits or lots of free time, and give up when their expectations aren't met.

3) Many businesses fail because they simply run out of **money** — entrepreneurs sometimes underestimate costs, or overestimate demand or sales, and the business fails because of a **cash flow** crisis (see p.34-35).

4) If a business has an **inaccurate** or **unrealistic** business plan to start with, it's likely to fail.

5) Unexpected delays or a lack of available supplies can cause a business to fail — this is **poor stock control**.

6) Not doing enough **market research**, or not making sure that the research is reliable can also be a cause of failure.

7) The wrong **location** can cause a business to fail, as can changing **market conditions**, such as a recession.

Practice Questions

Q1 Why does the government encourage entrepreneurs to start their own businesses?

Q2 Give three personal characteristics of a successful entrepreneur.

Q3 Why is it important to get the price of a product right?

Q4 Give three reasons why a new business might fail.

Exam Question

Q1 Johan Möller has invented a new tin-opener, and he is setting up his own business to make and sell it.
(a) Outline two difficulties that Johan will face in setting up his business. (4 marks)
(b) Discuss where Johan might get help with setting up his business. (4 marks)

All you need is an idea... and lots of research... and the right attitude...

Starting a new business sounds like a great idea — you get to be your own boss, and hopefully make loads of money to spend on fast cars and bling. But it can be scary — there are an awful lot of things to be responsible for. It seems that entrepreneurs have to do a heck of a lot of legwork to find out what the market's like and what they need to do to succeed.

New Business Ideas

Before setting up a business, entrepreneurs need to be sure their ideas will make money. If they don't have any business ideas, they could open a franchise. ***Page 8 is for AQA, WJEC and Edexcel, and page 9 is for AQA, WJEC and OCR.***

Entrepreneurs can target **Niche** or **Mass Markets**

1) Some products are aimed at a **mass market** — they're designed to appeal to **lots of consumers**, e.g. Coca-Cola®.
2) Other goods may be aimed at a **niche market** — a **smaller**, **more specific** group of consumers. E.g. a new fishing bait won't appeal to most people, but it could make a good **profit** if it sold well to fishermen.
3) **Small businesses** can be more successful if they focus on **niche markets** — it's easier than competing **directly** with large businesses. **Large manufacturers** don't normally bother with niche markets, so small businesses have a better chance of **success** if they target niche markets. E.g. if an entrepreneur wants to set up a small business selling microwave meals, it's a good idea to **establish a niche** by **specialising** in, say, meals for people with nut allergies — this will allow the firm to make a profit even though there are lots of large ready-meal businesses. It's also easier for small manufacturers to meet the demand of a small segment of the market.

Entrepreneurs need to **Know the Market**

There's more on niche and mass markets on p10 and more on market segmentation on p.80.

1) Entrepreneurs need good **background knowledge** of the market they want to sell to — it's easier to know what will sell well in a particular market if you have **personal experience** of that market. E.g. if you don't know about dancing it's probably a bad idea to design a new dancing shoe — you won't know what dancers want or need.
2) When they're designing a new product, entrepreneurs need to check if any **similar products** are already on the market — otherwise they could waste time inventing something that's **already** been invented, or developing a product that's **less suitable** than what's already available. If there are plenty of competitors in the market already, there might not be any demand for a new product unless it's offering something different.

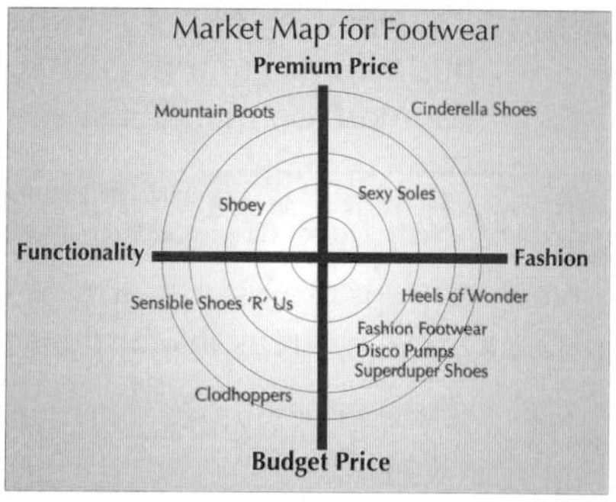
Market Map for Footwear
Premium Price
Mountain Boots
Cinderella Shoes
Sexy Soles
Shoey
Functionality
Fashion
Heels of Wonder
Sensible Shoes 'R' Us
Fashion Footwear
Disco Pumps
Superduper Shoes
Clodhoppers
Budget Price

3) **Market mapping** is one way a company can find out if there's a **gap in the market** for a particular business idea. The market map on the right shows how existing shoe shops might vary in terms of the **price** of their product and how **fashionable** it is. However, companies need to be careful with market mapping— they shouldn't assume that just because there are a lot of companies on one area of the map, that they shouldn't launch a similar product. E.g. there are a lot of firms selling high fashion shoes at low prices because there's a lot of demand for that kind of product.
4) Just because a product hasn't been invented yet **doesn't** mean it'll be commercially successful — some things simply aren't profitable, or won't catch on even if they're original. To get a feel for how successful their idea will be, entrepreneurs can carry out market research (see p.82-83).

Original **Ideas** can be **Protected** by law

AQA and Edexcel

Businesses and individuals who produce **original work** and earn an income through it need to **protect their ideas** from being copied by others. There are several ways of protecting ideas, depending on what is being protected:

1) A patent is a way of registering and protecting a new invention

If you have a new invention, you can apply for a **patent** from the **Patent Office** (a government agency that checks that an invention is an original design). If you have a patent for your **product**, or your **method** for producing it, no one else can copy it unless you give them a **licence** — and you can **charge** for the licence.

2) Trademarks (™) protect logos and slogans

If you want to protect your business' name, logo or slogan, you can register it as a **trademark** (™) so that nobody else can use it. E.g. the McDonald's golden arches logo is the **intellectual property** of the McDonald's Corporation and it can't be used by any other company. McDonald's promote a certain **brand image** — if the logo was used by other companies, McDonald's **reputation** might be damaged. McDonald's might also lose **profits** if consumers went to another restaurant by mistake because it had the same logo.

3) Copyright gives protection to written work and music

It's **illegal** to reproduce other people's work without their permission. Authors and musicians or their publishers receive payments called **royalties** every time their work is published or played on the radio.

AQA and Edexcel
AQA and Edexcel

Franchises

This page is for AQA, WJEC and OCR.

Franchises are **Special Agreements** between **One Business** and **Another**

1) Franchises aren't really a type of business ownership as such. They're **agreements** (contracts) which allow one business to use the **business idea**, **name** and **reputation** of another business.

2) The **franchisor** is the business which is willing to sell, or license, the use of its idea, name and reputation. The **franchisee** is the business which wants to use the name.

3) Several well-known retail chains in the UK operate as franchises, e.g. KFC, Burger King, McDonald's, Pizza Hut and The Body Shop®.

The franchisee gets benefits from running a franchise business:

1) A **well-known name**.

2) A **successful** and **proven** business idea — there is **less risk** of a franchise failing than a totally new business

3) **Training** and **financial support** to set up a new franchise outlet.

4) **Marketing**, **advertising** and **promotion** are done **nationally** by the franchisor.

5) **Buying** is done **centrally** by the franchisor — this helps franchise **outlets** keep **costs** down.

6) Expensive equipment can be **leased** from the franchisor.

7) It can be **easier to finance** a business if it's a franchise — banks can be **more willing** to lend money to people who want to buy a franchise from an established franchisor rather than set up a business from scratch.

There are some drawbacks for the franchisee:

1) They have to **pay** the franchisor for the right to use the name.

2) They have to pay the franchisor part of the **profits** or an **agreed sum**.

3) They have to run the business according to the franchisor's **rules** — they can't choose their own decor, etc.

4) It might be difficult to **sell** the franchise — they can only sell it to someone the franchisor approves of.

5) The franchise could get a **bad reputation** if other franchisees give bad customer service or sell sub-standard goods.

The franchisor gets benefits from franchising their business:

1) **Someone** else **runs** part of their business for them, so they **save money** on **wages**.

2) They get **paid** for the use of their **name**, and they get a **share of the profits**.

3) The more franchises there are, the faster the **name** of the business can be **spread**.

4) The **risk** involved in opening an outlet in a new location is **reduced** because the franchisee takes on some of the risk.

There are some drawbacks for the franchisor, too:

1) They have to **help** the franchisee set up a new franchise, which takes time.

2) They provide a **good business concept**, but they have to **share the rewards** with the franchisee.

3) If their franchisees don't have good standards, the franchisor's brand could get a **bad reputation**.

Practice Questions

Q1 What's the difference between a mass market and a niche market?

Q2 How can entrepreneurs legally protect new inventions? — *Questions 2 & 3 are for AQA and Edexcel only.*

Q3 What's the purpose of copyright?

Q4 What's meant by the terms "franchisee" and "franchisor"?

Exam Question

Q1 Evaluate the advantages and disadvantages of franchising, for both the franchisor and the franchisee. *(4 marks)*

I always thought patents were just really shiny leather shoes...

There's lots to learn on these pages, but don't let that get you down — just keep going over all the information until you're sure you've learnt it all. You need to know how entrepreneurs identify and protect a gap in the market, and understand how franchises work — don't forget to learn the advantages and disadvantages for the franchisee and franchisor too.

Understanding Markets

Businesses usually make a profit if they provide products that customers want or need. That's why, if they want to be successful, they really need to understand the market they're trying to sell to. **These pages are for all boards.**

Markets are where Sales Happen — they aren't Limited to a Physical Place

The market is where the buyer and seller meet. Traditionally the term "**market**" meant the physical **place** where people traded their goods — now it can mean **websites** like eBay™. "Market" also describes the **type** of **product or service** being bought and sold — e.g. the leisure market, the computer hardware market, the global oil market.

1) **Niche markets** serve **specialist consumers**. They can give **high profit margins** — there can be a big **difference** between what it **costs** to make something and what the business can **sell** it for.

2) **Mass markets** sell ordinary things to very large numbers of people at quite cheap prices. Businesses can get **high volume sales** but at a fairly **low profit margin**. (There's more about niche and mass markets on p.8.)

3) **Industrial markets** are where businesses sell to other businesses, such as wholesalers supplying retailers.

4) **Consumer markets** are where firms sell to individual customers — e.g. high street shops like Currys and Next.

5) **Local markets** are where firms sell to customers who live nearby. Selling to a **national market** means selling to people who live all over the country.

6) **Electronic markets** are **virtual markets** where customers don't physically interact with sellers — instead, buying and selling is done over the internet through websites like eBay™. Firms in electronic markets that sell to other companies are called "**business-to-business**" (B2B) companies, and the ones that sell to individual customers are called "**business-to-consumer**" (B2C) companies.

The Success of a business depends on Demand

Businesses try to increase their market share (see p.81) by increasing **demand** for their products among consumers. If demand for their products increases, they'll sell more products and make bigger profits. Several factors affect demand — some of these can be controlled by the business but others can't. The main factors affecting demand are:

1) The **price of the product**. As price goes up, the demand tends to go down — as price goes down, demand goes up.

2) The **actions of competitors**. When one manufacturer increases its prices, demand for **cheaper competitor products** tends to **rise**.

3) **Customer income**. When people have **more money** to spend, there's more demand.

4) **Seasonality**. E.g. the demand for ice cream is greater in the **summer**.

5) **Marketing**. Successful marketing (e.g. a TV advertising campaign or a "buy one get one free" offer) stimulates demand.

Nobody was sure which was falling faster — Jim, or demand for tiny, fluorescent swimming trunks.

The Supply of a product depends on Profitability and Demand — not for AQA

1) Businesses try to increase **demand** for their products, but this is only helpful if they can **supply** enough products to meet customer demand.

2) The term "supply" doesn't mean the quantity of products that are actually sold to customers — it's the quantity that businesses are **willing** to offer for sale, and **able** to produce.

3) With certain goods, **supply** tends to **increase** as the **price** that people are willing to pay **increases** — existing suppliers will be encouraged to supply more if they can make bigger profits, and new competitors will also be attracted into the market. If the **price** of goods **decreases**, **supply** often goes **down**. This is especially true for **commodities** (products which are of a similar quality no matter where they come from (e.g. sugar, rubber, wool).

4) For other products, such as electrical goods, **supply** tends to **increase** even when the **price falls**. E.g. the price of MP3 players decreases over time once companies have paid off the cost of research and development and more competitors have entered the market, but this causes **demand** to **increase**, so **supply increases** too.

5) **Supply** is also affected by the **cost** of supplying products. If the **cost** of labour or raw materials goes **up**, the business' profit margin **decreases** at the current price, so the business is less willing to supply the product. On the other hand, if the production **costs** go **down**, the product will be more **profitable** at the current price, so the business will be willing to **increase supply**.

6) If there's excess supply (**supply** is far **greater** than **demand**), **prices** will **fall**. If there's a shortage of supply (**demand** is far **greater** than **supply**), **prices** will **rise**.

not for AQA

not for AQA

not for AQA

Understanding Markets

Demand and Supply affect a product's Price and the Quantity sold

The diagram shows the relationship between **demand** and **supply**, and how they affect the **price** and **quantity sold**.

1)   **Demand** (the quantity that buyers will buy at a particular price) usually **increases** as the **price decreases** (the price elasticity of demand shows **how much** the demand changes with price — see p. 92-93). If the product is **cheaper**, it's logical that **more people** will **want** to and be **able** to buy it.

2)   **Supply** (the quantity of products that producers are willing and able to produce) **increases** as the **price increases** — producers like higher prices because they mean bigger profits.

3)   In a **free market**, demand and supply determine the **equilibrium price**. The equilibrium price is the price where the **quantity demanded** is equal to the **quantity supplied** (where the **demand** and **supply** curves **meet** on the graph).

4)   When there's too much supply or too much demand, the market is in **disequilibrium** — out of balance. Markets in disequilibrium **move back** towards equilibrium. This is because when the price is **too high**, there aren't enough customers willing to buy the products, so there's excess supply and sellers **cut prices** to increase demand. When the price is **too low**, there's too much demand for a limited supply so buyers will be willing to pay more and the **price rises** back to the equilibrium level.

5)   Sometimes **demand** for a product **changes** even when the price stays the same, e.g. due to a successful **marketing** campaign or a change in consumer income levels. This **shifts** the demand curve **outwards** (if demand increases) or **inwards** (if demand decreases) and there is a **new** equilibrium price and quantity.

6)   An outward shift (representing an increase in demand) is shown on the diagram — the supply curve stays the same but the demand curve **shifts** outwards. At the initial price, there would no longer be enough supply to meet demand, so the **equilibrium** price and quantity **increase**.

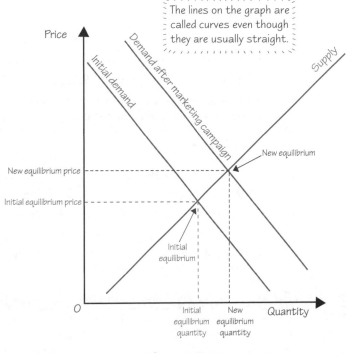

The lines on the graph are called curves even though they are usually straight.

not for AQA   *not for AQA*

Practice Questions

Q1   Name three different types of markets.
Q2   How does customer income affect demand?
Q3   What is the relationship between supply and price?
Q4   What is meant by the term "equilibrium price"?
Q5   Give two examples of factors other than customer income that can cause a shift in the demand curve.
Q6   What causes an outward shift in the demand curve?

Exam Questions

Q1   Describe the process of reaching an equilibrium price. (8 marks)

Q2   Priya is planning to open an ice cream shop in a seaside town which already has two other ice cream shops. Discuss some of the factors that might affect the demand for her products. (8 marks)

Did you know — agoraphobia is literally "fear of the marketplace"...

...and although there are a lot of different kinds of market out there, you don't need to be frightened of any of them. Demand and supply are the most important things on these pages, so make sure you understand the factors that affect them. You need to know what causes disequilibrium, and how businesses find the equilibrium price and quantity too.

Choosing a Suitable Legal Structure

If you're setting up your own business you need to choose the right type of legal structure for it — each type of structure has benefits and drawbacks. It's quite complicated, but the next few pages will help you work out what's what. **These pages are for AQA, OCR, Edexcel and WJEC.**

Sole Trader Businesses are run by an Individual

1) A sole trader is an **individual** trading in his or her own name, or under a suitable trading name. Sole traders are **self-employed**, for example as shopkeepers, plumbers, electricians, hairdressers or consultants.

2) The essential feature of this type of business is that the sole trader has **full responsibility** for the **financial control** of his or her own business and for meeting **running costs** and **capital requirements**. Having full responsibility for all the **debts** of the business is called **unlimited liability**.

3) There are **minimal legal formalities** — the trader simply has to start trading. However, if the business isn't run under the **proprietor's** (owner's) name, the trader has to **register** the company name under the Business Names Act (1985).

'Capital' just means 'money'. 'Capital requirement' is money invested to set up a business or fund growth.

4) There are several **advantages** to being a sole trader:

- **Freedom** — the sole trader is his/her **own boss** and has complete **control** over decisions.
- **Profit** — the sole trader is entitled to **all the profit** made by the business.
- **Simplicity** — there's **less form-filling** than for a limited company. Bookkeeping is less complex.
- **Savings on fees** — there aren't any legal costs like you'd get with drawing up a partnership agreement or limited company documentation.

5) There are **disadvantages** too:

- **Risk** — there's **no one** to share the **responsibilities** of running the business with.
- **Time** — sole traders often need to work **long hours** to meet tight deadlines.
- **Expertise** — the sole trader may have **limited skills** in areas such as finance.
- **Vulnerability** — there's **no cover** if the trader gets **ill** and can't work.
- **Unlimited liability** — the sole trader is **responsible** for all the debts of the business.

A Partnership is a Group of Individuals working together

1) Examples of partnerships include groups of doctors, dentists, accountants and solicitors.

2) The law allows a partnership to have between **two** and **twenty partners**, although some **professions**, e.g. accountants and solicitors, are allowed **more** than twenty.

3) A partnership can either trade in the **names** of the partners, or under a suitable **trading name**.

4) Partnerships need rules. Most partnerships operate according to the terms of a **partnership agreement** (also called a **deed of partnership**). This is a document drawn up by a **solicitor** which sets out:

- The amount of **capital** contributed by each partner.
- The procedure in case of **partnership disputes**.
- How the **profit** will be shared between partners.
- Partners' **voting rights**.
- The procedures for **bringing in new partners** and old partners retiring.

There are **advantages** to a partnership:	There are **disadvantages** to a partnership:
1) More owners bring **more capital** to invest at start-up.	1) Partners still have **unlimited liability**.
2) Partners can bring **more ideas** and **expertise** to a partnership.	2) Each partner is liable for **decisions** made by **other partners** — even if they had **no say** in the decision.
3) Partners can **cover** for each other's **holidays** and **illness**.	3) There's a **risk** of **conflict** between partners.

Choosing a Suitable Legal Structure

Liability to pay off Business Debts can be Limited or Unlimited

Sole traders and partnerships have unlimited liability

1) The **business** and the **owner** are **seen as one** under the **law**.

2) This means **business debts** become the **personal debts** of the owner. Sole traders and partners can be forced to **sell personal assets** like their **house** to pay off business debts.

3) Unlimited liability is a **huge financial risk** — it's an important factor to consider when deciding on the type of ownership for a new business.

When Louise's clothes-designing business failed, unlimited liability became a real pain.

Limited liability is a much smaller risk

1) Limited liability means that the owners **aren't personally responsible** for the debts of the business.

2) The **shareholders** of both **private** and **public limited companies** (see p. 14) have limited liability, because a limited company has a **separate legal identity** from its owners.

3) The **most** the shareholders in a limited company can lose is the money they have **invested** in the company.

In a limited company, the shareholders own the business.

The difference between limited liability and unlimited liability is **really important**. Say, for example, that someone puts **£1500** into their own business. The business hits bad times, and eventually goes bankrupt, owing **£20 000**. If the owner is a **sole trader**, he or she is liable to pay the **full amount**. If they're a **shareholder** of a limited company, they only lose the **£1500** they put in.

Some Partners in a partnership can have Limited Liability

1) The Limited Partnership Act (1907) allows a **partnership** to claim **limited liability** for **some** of its partners.

2) The partners with limited liability are called **sleeping partners**.

3) Sleeping partners can put **money** into the partnership but they **aren't allowed** to do anything to **run** the business.

4) There must be at least one **general partner** who is fully **liable** for all **debts** and obligations of the partnership.

Practice Questions

Q1 What legal requirements does a sole trader have to fulfil before he or she can start trading?

Q2 What's the maximum number of partners allowed in a dental practice?

Q3 What's the difference between limited liability and unlimited liability?

Q4 Which represents the biggest risk to the owners of a business — limited liability or unlimited liability?

Q5 Under what circumstances can partners in a partnership have limited liability?

Exam Question

Q1 Eric, a plumber trading as a sole trader, wants to go into partnership with his friend Sandra (also a plumber). Explain why he might want to change the type of ownership of his business. Evaluate the implications of doing so. (12 marks)

Sole traders — they're not just shoemakers...

They can also be plumbers, window cleaners, greengrocers — you get the idea. Anyway, the important thing to remember here is that sole traders and partnerships both have unlimited liability, so if you're going to set up one of these types of businesses you need to be pretty sure that it's not going to fail. Otherwise you're in big trouble.

Choosing a Suitable Legal Structure

Companies are different from sole traders and partnerships — they only have limited liability, for a start. **For all boards.**

There are two kinds of Limited Liability Companies — Ltds and PLCs

1) There are **private limited companies** and **public limited companies**.
2) Public and private limited companies have **limited liability** (see p.13).
3) They're owned by **shareholders** and run by **directors**.
4) The **capital value** (see p.12) of the company is **divided** into **shares** — these can be **bought** and **sold** by shareholders.
5) Both require a minimum of only two shareholders, and there's no upper limit on the number of shareholders.

More on shares on p.19.

Private Limited Companies	Public Limited Companies
Can't sell shares to the public. People in the company own all the shares.	Can sell shares to the **public**. They must issue a **prospectus** to inform people about the company before they buy.
Don't have share prices quoted on **stock exchanges**.	Their share prices can be quoted on the **Stock Exchange**.
Shareholders may not be able to sell their shares without the **agreement** of the **other shareholders**.	Shares are **freely transferable** and can be bought and sold through stockbrokers, banks and share shops.
They're often **small** family businesses.	They usually **start** as **private** companies and then go **public later** to raise more capital.
There's **no minimum share capital** requirement.	They need **over £50 000** of share capital, and if they're listed on a stock exchange, **at least 25%** of this must be publicly available. People in the company can own the rest of the shares.
They end their name with the word "limited" or **Ltd**.	They always end their name with the initials **PLC**.

Companies are governed by the Companies Act (1985)

The Companies Act (1985) says that two important documents must be drawn up **before** a company can start trading. These are the **memorandum of association** and the **articles of association**.

Memorandum of Association

1) The **memorandum of association** gives the company name followed by **Ltd**, if it's a private limited company, or **PLC**, if it's a public limited company, and it gives the company's business address.
2) The memorandum of association says what the **objectives** of the company are.
3) It gives **details** of the company's capital, e.g. £250 000 divided into 250 000 Ordinary Shares of £1 each.
4) It states clearly that the **shareholders' liability is limited**.

Articles of Association

1) The **articles of association** are the **internal rules** of the company.
2) They give the **names** of the **directors**.
3) They say **how directors are appointed** and what kind of **power** they have.
4) The articles of association say what the **shareholders' voting rights** are.
5) They set out when and how the company will hold **shareholders' meetings**.
6) The articles of association set out how the company will **share** its **profits**.

Companies House is where records of all UK companies are kept.

The **memorandum of association** and **articles of association** must both be sent to **Companies House**.
The Registrar of Companies issues a **certificate of incorporation** so that the company can start trading.
Once it's up and running, the company is legally obliged to produce **annual reports** of its financial activities.

Companies are controlled by Shareholders and Directors

1) All the shareholders in a **small** private limited company are usually the **directors**. The shareholders who hold the **most shares** have the **most power**.
2) In larger private limited companies, directors are **elected** to the board by **shareholders**. The board makes the important decisions. **Shareholders vote** on the performance of the board at the Annual General Meeting (**AGM**).
3) Shares in a PLC can be owned by **anyone**. The people who **own** the company (the shareholders) don't necessarily **control** the company — it's **controlled** by the **directors**. This is called the "**divorce of ownership and control**".

Choosing a Suitable Legal Structure

Not-for-Profit businesses are another type of business structure

1) As their name suggests, not-for-profit businesses are **not** set up to make a **profit**. Instead, they have other aims, often to **help** people or benefit the community.

2) **Not-for-profit** businesses are run in a similar way to other businesses. They usually have money coming in and going out — the main difference is that the money generated by the business **doesn't** go to the owners or shareholders as **profit**.

3) **Public-sector** organisations like the NHS and the fire service are not-for-profit businesses. Public sector organisations are run in a similar way to other businesses, but they don't charge for their services so they don't make a profit — they're funded by the UK **tax system**.

*National and local governments use money from taxes to provide **merit goods** (things they think we need) like healthcare, and **public goods** (things that we all use) like street lighting.*

4) **Charities** like the Red Cross and Oxfam are also not-for-profit businesses — they make money from **donations** and business activities (like charity shops), but this money is used to fund charitable activities, e.g. setting up hospitals in developing countries. Charities get **tax reductions** because of their not-for-profit structure.

5) Many **local organisations** and societies are run as not-for-profit businesses — e.g. amateur theatre groups might charge for tickets to see their performances, but the money generated from ticket sales is put back into the business, to cover the costs of renting a building for the performance, buying costumes, etc.

Entrepreneurs have to Choose a Legal Structure for their business

1) When someone sets up a business, they have to **decide** whether to set up as a sole trader, a partnership, a private limited company (Ltd.) or a public limited company (PLC). Each of the business structures has **advantages** and **disadvantages** — the entrepreneur has to decide which is most **suitable** for their needs.

2) Setting up a **sole trader** business gives the owner **control** over the business, but **unlimited liability** is a drawback. It's a **simple** way to set up a small business, but there's a lot of **risk** involved for the owner.

3) A **partnership** means more people with more **money** and more **ideas**, but there's a risk of **disagreements** between partners and there's still **unlimited liability**.

4) A **private limited company** (Ltd.) has **limited liability** and the shareholders keep **control** over who other shares are sold to, but it's much more **complicated** to set up than a sole trader business.

5) **Public limited companies** aren't usually a suitable option for new businesses because they need at least **£50 000** of share capital to start with, and most new businesses can't raise that much money.

6) Businesses can **change** their structure — sole traders can join together to form a partnership, or they can become a private limited company if they want to **expand**. Lots of private limited companies become PLCs when they want to raise more money to expand the business.

7) It's much less common, but **PLCs** can also become private limited companies if they are **taken over** by a **private limited company** or if the managers **buy out** the **shareholders**. For example, in 2002, Arcadia Group PLC was taken over by Phillip Green's private limited company Taveta Investment Ltd. and is now Arcadia Group Ltd.

Practice Questions

Q1 State two differences between private and public limited companies.
Q2 Give three examples of not-for-profit businesses.
Q3 Why are new businesses not usually set up as PLCs?

Exam Question

Q1 Ogen Organics is a family-owned private limited company selling organic make-up and toiletries. The business has been growing over the past few years and one of the directors suggests becoming a PLC. Discuss the advantages and disadvantages of doing this. (6 marks)

All this legal stuff seemed much more entertaining on Ally McBeal...

It's a bit of a pain having to learn all the legal ins and outs of different business structures, but make sure you do because this is quite likely to crop up in the exam. You might be asked to decide whether a particular business would be better off as a sole trader, partnership, private limited company or PLC, so you need to be able to choose between them.

Location

When you're deciding where to set up a business, it's all about location, location, location.
These pages are for AQA and WJEC.

Businesses use **Cost-Benefit Analysis** to choose a **Location**

1) **Cost-benefit analysis** means **weighing** up the **costs** of an opportunity against its potential **benefits**.

2) Renting or buying somewhere is a big **investment** for a business. When deciding where to locate, businesses consider how each location will affect **costs** and **revenues** (e.g. rents and labour costs in Newcastle are likely to be lower than rents and labour costs in London). Businesses use **quantitative analysis** techniques such as **break-even analysis** to measure this (see p. 32-33).

3) Businesses calculate how many sales they'll need to break even (see p.32) at each potential location. Where the **costs of operating** from a location are **high**, the amount of goods a company needs to produce to **break-even** will be higher. It's better to put your business in a location where break-even output is low.

Businesses make **Location** decisions based on **Practical** factors

The best location for a business depends on several factors, and is different for different types of business.

Transport costs affect where businesses are located

1) **Manufacturing** businesses which provide **bulky finished products** should be located near to their **customers** to cut down on distribution costs. Bulky products made from **lightweight** components are called "**bulk increasing**" goods.

2) Other products need **bulky raw materials** to make a **lightweight end product** — these are "**bulk decreasing**" goods. They need to be located near the source of **raw materials** to keep transport costs down.

3) A good **transport infrastructure** (see below) cuts distribution costs.

4) **Services** don't have large distribution costs. Decisions on where to locate services are based mainly on other criteria.

> E.g. beer — made of water (available anywhere), plus hops and barley (low in bulk compared to the finished product). Breweries tend to be located near consumers and transport infrastructure, not near hop or barley fields.

> E.g. a small business producing bottled mineral water is likely to be based near the source of the water — otherwise it would be very expensive to transport the water to the bottling factory.

A good location needs a good infrastructure

1) Businesses benefit from access to **motorways**, fast **rail** links, **sea ports** and **airports**.

2) Transport infrastructure is needed for the **import** of **raw materials**, the **distribution** of **finished products**, and for **staff** to get to work.

3) Businesses also need **support services**. Most business organisations need some form of **commercial** support such as **banking**, **insurance** and **marketing** agencies.

4) They often need **technical** support such as engineering services and **IT** assistance.

Businesses need a location with good land and labour resources

1) There must be a **good supply** of labour resources in the area where a business will be located.

2) The labour force must also be **suitable** — they might need special skills like IT, technical knowledge, etc.

3) The area might need **local training facilities** for staff, e.g. a college or university.

4) The area needs **facilities** such as affordable housing, suitable schooling, medical facilities and retail and leisure outlets to provide a good **quality of life** for staff.

5) Businesses also need the right land resources. They might need space to **expand** in the future.

6) The **cost** of **land** and **property** for factories and business premises varies significantly from area to area — land in the London area is far more expensive than land in mid-Wales, for example.

7) Businesses can pay workers **less** in areas where the **cost of living** is lower. In a **global economy**, businesses can market their products all over the world, so they can produce products in countries with **cheap labour costs** and sell them in the rest of the world. E.g. many UK banks have moved their call centres to India where labour costs are lower than in the UK.

Location decisions depend on the market

1) Some businesses such as **retailers** need to locate **near to customers**, in order to catch the passing trade.

Location

The Government provides Incentives to locate in certain areas

Governments try to attract businesses to areas with high **unemployment**. They use both "**carrots**" (e.g. giving **grants** to businesses locating in areas of high unemployment) and "**sticks**" (e.g. **refusing planning permission** to build a factory in an area where there are already lots of jobs) to encourage businesses to locate in deprived areas.

In 1998, the UK government set up 8 **Regional Development Agencies** (RDAs) to coordinate and encourage development. They can provide **financial assistance** to businesses through grants, loans and equity (share) investment. They provide **financial** and **management advice**, and can help businesses find the right location.

As another part of its regional policy, the UK government has also named certain less economically developed parts of the country as **assisted areas**. Within these areas government **grants** are available to persuade manufacturing and service businesses to locate there. Cornwall and the Scottish Highlands are two examples of assisted areas.

There are also Qualitative Factors involved in Choosing a Location

1) Decisions about where to base a business are not always just based on things that can be **measured**.

2) Entrepreneurs might choose to start a business near where they **live**.

3) Some places have a **good image** which suits the image of the product. High fashion works better in New York, London and Paris than in Scunthorpe — New York, London and Paris already have a fashionable image.

Businesses don't usually find an Ideal Location

1) All these factors rarely, if ever, combine in one place to create an **ideal** location. It's more likely that the decision of where to locate a business is based on a **compromise** between different factors.

2) Small businesses don't usually have much **choice** about which area of the country to locate in — entrepreneurs don't usually have spare cash to move location, so they tend to set up the business in the area where they already live. They still have to decide whereabouts in the town/city to locate though — e.g. someone thinking of opening a coffee shop might choose to set up close to a university to attract students.

3) Small businesses can be at a **disadvantage** because they might not be able to afford the best location — e.g. an entrepreneur setting up a clothes shop might not be able to afford the rent in the city centre, so their shop might be in a side street where fewer people pass by.

4) **Modern technology** means that many businesses can be more **flexible** about their location. Businesses that trade over the internet rather than face-to-face can be based anywhere in the world. Doing business over the internet can be a useful way for entrepreneurs who don't live in big cities to reach customers.

Businesses may have to Relocate — move facilities somewhere else

1) Established businesses sometimes have to **move**. This may be because the business has grown **too large** for its premises, or because **government incentives** have been **withdrawn**, or **taxes** have **risen**.

2) Deciding where to relocate is similar to deciding where to locate, but with some added **problems**. **Production** is likely to be reduced during the move. **Staff** may not want to move and you might have to **pay** them to relocate. It's also **expensive** to notify customers and suppliers, update brochures and headed notepaper, etc.

Practice Questions

Q1 Identify and briefly explain three factors which affect location cost.

Q2 What are assisted areas?

Q3 Why is it difficult for small businesses to find an ideal location?

Exam Question

Q1 What factors should an entrepreneur consider when deciding where to locate a restaurant business? (10 marks)

Phil and Kirstie can't help you now...

You're going to have to learn the factors that affect business location, no maybes about it. If this comes up in the exam (more than likely) you'll probably get a case study with some facts and figures about a business, and you'll be asked to say why the business chose to locate where it did. Or you might have to write a report recommending a location for a business.

Financing a Business

All businesses need finance. There are loads of possible sources of finance — businesses just have to find the right one.
These pages are for AQA, OCR, Edexcel and WJEC.

It **Costs** a lot to **Start** and **Run** a business

1) New businesses **can't** usually **put off** paying costs like employees' wages, rent on business premises and the costs of equipment and raw materials. This is a **problem** because money won't start coming into the business until much **later**, when the business starts being **paid** for its products.

2) If the business **can't** pay what it owes in time, it will have to **close down**.

3) To make sure that the business will **survive** until revenue starts coming in, and to pay all the **bills** once the business starts trading, the entrepreneur needs to find a way of **financing** the business.

4) Most entrepreneurs use some of their **own** money to finance their business, but very few have enough savings to cover all the costs — they have to find other ways of financing the business.

5) Established businesses also need finance to buy fixed assets or for day-to-day running costs.

Established Businesses can raise Internal Capital *(from within the business)*

not AQA

1) Businesses can save their **trading profit** to use for **later investment** — this is called **retained profit**.

2) A business can find some internal capital by **reducing working capital** (money needed for the basic running of the business). They do this by reducing the amount of **stock** they hold, **delaying** payments to **suppliers** and **speeding up** payments from **customers**. The amount of capital a business can get from doing this is **limited**.

3) Firms can **sell** some of their **assets**, e.g. part of their premises, to generate capital. This is called **rationalisation**.

not AQA ——— *not AQA* ——— *not AQA*

External Finance can be for Short-, Medium- and Long-Term Needs

External finance can increase working capital in the short term

1) **Trade credit** is where a business negotiates a **delay** between **receiving** raw materials or stock and **paying** for them. **30 days** is a typical credit period. Larger businesses may negotiate longer periods.

2) **Overdrafts** can be used for short-term finance.

External finance is used for medium-term needs — usually between 1 and 5 years

1) **Loans** are suitable for **medium-term** finance.

2) **Leasing** is when a business **rents** fixed assets like cars and office equipment instead of **buying** them. Leasing means paying a smallish amount each month instead of shelling out a lot of money all in one go. In the **long run**, leasing works out **more expensive** than buying, though.

External finance can also be used for long-term projects

1) **Debentures** are a special kind of long-term **loan** with low **fixed interest rates** and **fixed repayment dates**.

2) **Grants** are money from central and local government and some business charities — they don't have to be repaid. To qualify for a grant, businesses usually have to be creating **new jobs**, setting up in **deprived** areas, etc.

3) **Venture capitalists** provide capital by giving loans and by buying shares. Venture capital is particularly suitable for business start-ups or expansion.

Businesses can use Overdrafts for Short-Term finance

1) **Overdrafts** are where a bank lets a business spend **more** money **than** it **has** in its account, up to a **limit**. The overspend is recorded as a **negative** figure.

2) Many businesses use overdrafts to cover some of their day-to-day costs, especially if they have **short-term** cash flow problems (see p.34-35). They're **not** suitable for **long-term** finance though.

Advantages of overdrafts	Disadvantages of overdrafts
1) They're **quick** and **easy** to set up — banks will usually offer them to anyone, unlike loans.	1) The interest rate is usually very **high** so they are **expensive** if they're used over long periods of time.
2) They're **flexible** — the business only has to pay interest on the amount that it actually borrows.	2) The bank can **remove** the overdraft facility at any time and demand all the money back.

Financing a Business

Businesses can take out Loans for Medium-Term finance

1) Businesses can get **loans** from **banks**. They borrow a fixed amount of **money** and pay it back over a fixed period of **time** with **interest** — the amount they pay back depends on the interest rate and the duration of the loan.

2) Loans are a good way of financing a business **start-up** and paying for **assets** like machinery and computers. They are **not** a good way to cover the **day-to-day** running costs of the business.

Advantages of bank loans

1) You're **guaranteed** the money for the duration of the loan (the bank can't suddenly demand it back).

2) You only have to pay back the **loan** and **interest** — the bank won't **own** any of your business and you don't have to give them a share of the **profits**.

3) The interest charges for a loan are usually **lower** than for an overdraft.

Disadvantages of bank loans

1) They can be **difficult** to arrange because the bank will only lend the business money if they think they're going to get it back. If the entrepreneur doesn't own any **property** or other assets that can be used for **security**, they might not be able to get a loan.

2) Keeping up with the **repayments** can be difficult if cash isn't coming into the business quickly enough. The entrepreneur might **lose** whatever the loan is secured on (e.g. their home).

3) The business might have to pay a **charge** if they decide to pay the loan back **early**.

Entrepreneurs may be able to borrow money from **friends** or **family** — they'll probably charge **less interest** than banks. They're also unlikely to ask for security for the loan, and might be more **flexible** about when repayments are made. However, if the business fails then the lender will **lose** the money that they lent to the entrepreneur — this could have a very negative effect on the **relationship** between the entrepreneur and the lender.

The types of finance available to a business depend on what kind of business it is — not all types of finance are suitable for all types of firm.

Limited companies can sell Shares to raise finance

1) **Private limited companies** can raise finance by selling **shares** in the business.

2) Entrepreneurs can sell shares to their **friends** and **family**, or to **venture capitalists** — professional investors who buy shares in new businesses that they think have the potential to be successful.

3) The drawback of selling shares rather than taking out a loan is that the entrepreneur no longer **owns** all of the business — they have to give the shareholders a share of the **profits**, and they also have to give them a **say** in how the business is run.

Sally tried using her feminine wiles, but nothing could persuade Steve to buy shares in her suede raincoat business.

Practice Questions

Q1 Explain why a new business needs finance.

Q2 What is the main drawback of borrowing money from friends and family?

Q3 What is the difference between an overdraft and a loan?

Q4 What is meant by the term "venture capitalist"?

Exam Questions

Q1	Discuss what type of finance might be suitable for financing the launch of a cyber-café business.	(6 marks)
Q2	Discuss the advantages and disadvantages of financing a new business using a bank loan.	(8 marks)

Unfortunately you can't sell shares in being slightly bored with BS...

I was planning on financing my business with £1 coins from the back of the sofa. Guess not, then. All kidding aside, it's worth knowing about the different kinds of finance that entrepreneurs can use to start up their business. Learn the advantages and disadvantages of different forms of finance and you'll be laughing if it comes up in the exam.

Employing People

Even the most brilliant entrepreneurs can't do all the work in a successful business themselves — they're going to need to take on more staff at some point. There are different ways of employing people, so sorting out staffing can be tricky. ***These pages are for AQA, OCR, Edexcel and WJEC.***

Small businesses need to *Consider* their *Staffing Needs*

Small businesses might need to increase or decrease their staffing levels in the following situations:

1) The business is **expanding** — businesses may need **extra staff** to cope with the increased workload.

2) **Demand** increases — the business might need **extra staff** to keep up with demand.

3) A change in **direction** — if a business decides to move into a new area (e.g. if a hair salon decides to start providing beauty treatments), new staff with new **expertise** might be required.

4) **Quiet periods** — having too high staff levels at these times can cause problems for a small business because they have to **pay** all their staff even if they don't really need them.

Staff can be *Full-Time* or *Part-Time*

Most small businesses employ mainly **full-time** staff (staff working 35 hours or more per week). However, full-time staff are not always the best option for small businesses. Employing **part-time** staff can be better in some circumstances:

Advantages of part-time staff

1) Employing part-time staff can **save** the business **money**. There's no point paying full-time staff to be at work all week if there's not enough work for them to do.

2) Businesses have more **flexibility** to manage **workloads** — the business can use part-time workers to cover times when the workload is greater due to higher demand.

3) Part-time staff may have a better **work/life balance** (a good split between working and leisure time) so they are less likely to take time off with stress, or take sick days. Employing part-time staff to deal with increased workloads also eases the **pressure** on full-time staff, so stress and absenteeism among full-time staff are also likely to be reduced.

4) A better work/life balance is likely to mean **happier** staff — this could lead to an increase in **productivity**.

5) If you increase the number of employees, you'll usually get a wider range of **skills** and experience in the workforce.

Disadvantages of part-time staff

1) It can be difficult to **find** good part-time workers, because most jobseekers are likely to be looking for **full-time** work.

2) Part-time employees can sometimes be less **dedicated** and **loyal** than full-time workers — they spend a lower proportion of their time working for the business so it's not such an important part of their life.

3) Part-time employees might not have as much **experience** of how the business works as full-time staff do.

4) The recruitment and training processes are **time-consuming** and **expensive** — it's only worth spending money on hiring part-time employees if you're sure they're going to save you money.

Businesses need to get the *Balance* right

1) Small businesses need to get the **balance** between part-time and full-time staff **right** — e.g. an entrepreneur who sets up a small shop might employ one full-time member of staff, and a part-time member of staff to work on Saturdays, when the shop is busiest.

2) When entrepreneurs start up new businesses, they might be **unsure** of how **busy** they will be, or how many employees they'll need to cope with **demand** — it's best to take on **part-time** staff until they are sure that demand will be high enough to need full-time workers.

3) **Job-sharing** is when two (or more) employees work **part-time** sharing the **same** job. They usually work on different days of the week or alternate weeks, and they share the responsibility and pay of the job. This can be a good way of allowing higher-level staff like **managers** to work part-time without disrupting business activities, although it needs careful planning.

Laura found balancing crockery on her feet much easier than balancing her staffing levels.

Employing People

Staff can be *Temporary* or *Permanent*

1) **Permanent** staff work for the business **permanently** — the business can only stop employing them by either **dismissing** them (if they behave badly or are incapable of doing their job) or making them **redundant** (if the business no longer needs anyone to do their job). It's **expensive** to make permanent employees redundant — the firm has to give them redundancy pay.

2) **Temporary** staff work for the business for a **fixed period** of time (e.g. 6 months) or on a **week by week** basis — the business can renew the employee's contract if extra staff are needed for longer than this.

3) A small business can employ **temporary** workers in **high-risk** periods when the business' future is uncertain — then they can easily **reduce** their number of employees without having to pay redundancy money.

4) Recruitment is an **expensive** process, so businesses often use **employment agencies** to find temporary staff — the agency advertises the job and finds a suitable candidate, and the business has to pay a fee to the agency. In this case, workers are employed by the **agency** rather than the business.

5) **Contractors** can be used if a business needs staff with **specialist** skills on a **short-term** basis. Contractors charge a set fee for doing a **specific job** for a limited period of time, and staff are employed by the **contractor** rather than the business. Businesses tend to use contractors for services such as gardening, cleaning, building work, IT support and security.

Attracting new employees is *Difficult* ——— AQA

1) Businesses invest a lot of time and money in their staff, so it's important to find the **right** employees.

2) It's hard for small businesses to find good employees because they have **limited resources** to spend on recruitment — e.g. advertising jobs in national newspapers and magazines may be the best way to reach the best potential employees, but it may be too expensive for a small business.

3) Small businesses also find it difficult to attract good candidates because they cannot offer the same **salaries** and **benefits** as larger companies with more resources.

4) Businesses also have to consider **legal issues** when recruiting new staff. It's **illegal** for businesses to **discriminate** against potential employees because of their age, gender, race, religion, sexual orientation or because they have a disability. If a business refused to employ someone on these grounds, candidates could take them to an **employment tribunal**, and the business might have to pay **compensation**.

Businesses can get *Advice* on *Employment Matters*

1) Getting staffing **wrong** causes big **problems** for small businesses — if they don't have **enough** staff they won't be able to meet **demand**, and **too many** staff will create unnecessary **costs** for the business.

2) Small businesses can get **free** expert advice from Business Link or the Small Business Advisor at their bank.

3) Business owners can get expert employment advice by joining the British Chambers of Commerce, the Federation of Small Businesses or the Institute of Directors — there's a membership **fee** for joining though.

4) Businesses can **pay** specialist **consultants** to advise them, but this is an **expensive** option for small businesses.

— AQA ———————————————————— AQA —

Practice Questions

Q1 Give three examples of situations that might require businesses to consider their staffing needs.

Q2 State two advantages and two disadvantages of part-time staff.

Q3 Name three potential sources of advice on employment matters.

Exam Question

Q1 Discuss the practical and legal difficulties for small businesses of finding and attracting good employees. (10 marks)

You could always employ a lookalike to sit the exam for you...

Employing people might be stressful for entrepreneurs, but it shouldn't be too much of a headache for you — as long as you know the difference between part-time, full-time, permanent and temporary staff, and learn the advantages and disadvantages of each, you should be able to sail through employment questions in the exam.

Corporate Objectives

Businesses set aims and objectives to provide long-term targets. On the way to a big target, they set lots of little targets to make sure they're on the right track. **These two pages are for OCR and Edexcel.**

Corporate Planning starts with Corporate Aims

1) **Corporate aims** are the long-term ambitions of a business — the reason the business exists. They're quite general, e.g. "to offer our customers the best value for money possible", and businesses use them to create a common **vision (or mission)** for all employees to work towards.

2) **Mission statements** are written descriptions of business aims which businesses use to **inform** stakeholders and **motivate** employees.

3) **Strategic objectives** are medium-term to long-term targets that businesses set to help them achieve corporate aims. They're set by **senior management**.

4) **Operational** (or **tactical**) **objectives** are targets for the day-to-day operations of the business, to make sure it meets its strategic objectives. Operational objectives are set by managers within each **department**.

5) **Individual objectives** are targets for each individual employee.

The hierarchy of objectives

Corporate aims and mission statement

↓

Strategic objectives

↓

Operational or tactical objectives

↓

Individual objectives

Objectives affect Decision-Making and Strategies

Business decisions have to **fit in** with corporate **objectives**. If they don't, there's **no point** in having objectives at all.

1) **Long-term corporate objectives** set the whole **direction** of a business. They affect the **big decisions** that senior managers make. They also govern the setting of operational objectives.

2) **Operational objectives** rule decision-making on the "shop floor" where the **actual work** is done.

A **strategy** is a **plan** for how to achieve objectives.

A strategy plans out the **tactics** that a business is going to use to meet its objectives.

Tactics are the **actual activities** that the business uses to **work towards** its objectives.

In the exam, if you're asked to evaluate business decisions, make sure you take note of the firm's objectives. If the objectives are vague and useless, they won't be able to make decisions that push the business in a clear direction.

Businesses can have Short-term and Long-term Objectives

Long-term objectives include things like long-term growth. **Short-term** objectives include things like short-term **survival** and making short-term **profit**.

Short-term Objectives — Businesses Can Lose Out in the Long Run

1) **Short-term objectives** usually need a business to **cut back** on all its long-term objectives.

2) For example, a business trying to increase on last year's profits might **cut** its **advertising** budget, stop its **training** programme, and cut back on its **product development** budget. At the end of the year it'd have **more profit** because of cutting all those **costs**, but it would have lost out on its other objectives.

3) Businesses are often **criticised** for being too concerned with **short-term gain**. Shareholders often want a **quick return** on their investment, or they'll take their money and go elsewhere. Businesses have to go for short-term profits or risk losing investors.

4) There should be a **balance** between short-term and long-term objectives.

Crisis Management — Businesses have to React to Sudden Changes

1) Businesses have to **switch** to **temporary short-term objectives** to cope with short-term crisis situations.

2) For example, a growth objective might cause **overtrading** and a cash flow crisis (see p.34) — not enough liquid assets available to pay the bills. In a **cash flow crisis**, a business should focus on **short-term survival** instead of medium-term expansion — managers need to find ways of improving cash flow, or the business will go under.

3) For another example, a business going for **profit maximisation** must be prepared to take a **temporary loss of profits** and invest heavily in **advertising** and **promotions** if a new competitor enters the market.

Corporate Objectives

Objectives can either Minimise Risk or Maximise Reward

1) If you want to win big, you have to take chances. Objectives and strategies that go for **high rewards** are usually the most **risky**. You need a **balance** between low-risk, low-reward strategies and high-risk, high-reward strategies.

2) Some businesses choose to go **all-out** for high **profits**, or high **growth**. They're willing to take a **gamble** in the hope of getting big gains. Other businesses choose to **play it safe**, and avoid the risk of making a loss.

3) Risk-taking is related to **business ownership**. Businesses where the owners have **unlimited liability** might shy away from taking big risks. If it all goes wrong, the owners are stuck with all the debts. Incorporated companies with **limited liability** have less to lose. They can take more **risky** actions and bring in higher rewards.

4) Managers in companies where the owners **aren't** the people who **run** the company can easily end up setting objectives that are in their **own interest**, instead of in the interest of the **owners** of the company. This is a problem with the **divorce of ownership and control** — see p.14.

Stakeholder Conflicts — you can't please everyone

1) The needs and wants of different stakeholder groups aren't always **compatible** with each other. Each group of stakeholders tends to concentrate on its **own interests** and wants things done its own way.

2) The main balance when making big decisions is between **short-term profit** and **social responsibility** (see p.28)

Profit is important

1) If a company doesn't make a profit, it'll be unable to **survive**. It won't be able to pay its **suppliers** or its **employees** — that's two major stakeholders right up the spout.

2) **Shareholders** need profit so that they can get their **dividends**. Shareholders may decide to sack the directors or sell their shares to someone else, if they aren't getting enough return.

Social responsibility is important too

1) Companies that ignore their social responsibilities can face problems. E.g. **polluting** the environment could **put consumers off**. The state might close down production or fine factories which cause the worst pollution.

2) Relocating production to **another country** with **cheaper labour** isn't usually seen as socially responsible because it leads to **job losses** in the UK and some factories abroad might use **sweatshops** or **child labour**. The **state** can intervene with **incentives** that cut the cost of staying in the UK — subsidised land and premises, **tax breaks** and so on.

A company will prioritise different stakeholder groups depending on the situation. E.g. employees may decide to go on **strike** if the company increases working hours to meet production targets. Striking makes their demands more **important** to the business.

Different stakeholder **groups** have **different demands** and interests. The company must try to satisfy as **many** groups as possible and **still survive financially**. It's not easy, but most firms manage it.

Stakeholders **don't always disagree** though — for example, making workers happy can actually help productivity and raise profits.

Practice Questions

Q1 What's the difference between an objective and a strategy?

Q2 Explain why a firm might follow short-term objectives which conflict with its long-term corporate objectives.

Q3 What is the risk to a company of ignoring its social responsibilities?

Exam Question

Q1 The directors of Struthers & McFarland Ltd are discussing whether to turn their plastics manufacturing business into a public limited company. Some directors are concerned that being a PLC will force them to focus on short-term profit.
(a) Why might Struthers & McFarland have to focus on short-term objectives instead of long-term ones? (3 marks)
(b) What effects might a focus on short-term profit have on the business? (9 marks)

Objectives are, like, your destination, man...

This objective-strategy-decision thing? Look at it this way — imagine you're driving from Birmingham to Glasgow. You need directions to tell you how to get to Glasgow, and you need to make sure you take the right exit on the motorway and avoid taking wrong turns. A short-term objective of really needing a pee would be met by pulling off into a service station.

Business Plans

Making a plan is pretty vital if you want a successful business. Entrepreneurs need to make a plan if they want to stand a chance of getting anyone to invest in the business or give them a loan. **For AQA, Edexcel and WJEC.**

A **Business Plan** sets out the **Objectives** of the business

A business plan is a document that states **what** the owner(s) want to do and **how** they intend to do it.
There are several reasons for writing a business plan before starting a business:

1) The main purpose of a business plan is usually to get financial backing for the business. A business plan shows the **financial risk** involved in setting up the business — this is important for potential **lenders** or **investors** who may want to help finance the start-up. Banks and venture capitalists will want to see a business plan before they'll think about investing.

2) Setting down all the plans for the business in a report helps the entrepreneur to assess the business' **strengths** and **weaknesses**, and allows them to see whether their idea is actually **realistic**. It also helps them to identify areas that they need to think about and plan more thoroughly.

3) The business plan is an important **management** tool — it gives details of business **objectives**, which the entrepreneur can compare with the **actual** performance of the business once it starts trading in order to track its progress. It also reminds the owner of the **ideas** they had before the business started.

Business plans are divided into **Sections**

Most business plans contain the following sections:

1) **Executive summary** — this is a general **overview** of the business which contains the **key points** from all the other sections. It's really important because if potential investors aren't impressed by the executive summary then they might not bother to read the rest of the business plan.

2) **Business summary** — what **type** of business the entrepreneur wants to set up, what **product(s)** or **service(s)** the business intends to provide, **why** it wants to provide them and what gives it a **competitive advantage**. It also includes the **legal structure** of the business, and the entrepreneur's vision for the **future** of the business.

> E.g. if the business is a **cookery school**, the service it offers would be **cookery lessons**, and it might also offer products like **recipe books** and **cooking equipment**.
>
> The entrepreneur might want to provide these things because there isn't a cookery school in the area and there is **demand** for cooking lessons due to the popularity of TV chefs like Jamie Oliver and Nigella Lawson.
>
> It's **competitive advantage** might be that it can **source** all its fresh **ingredients locally**.
>
> The entrepreneur might be a **sole trader**, or the business could be a **partnership** or **limited company**.
>
> The entrepreneur's vision for the **future** might be:
>
> (a) to have a **revenue** of **£30 000** in the third year of trading,
>
> (b) to attract customers from all over the **UK** for cooking holidays as well as holding classes for **local** people,
>
> (c) to eventually open a **bed-and-breakfast** where students on the holiday courses can stay.

3) **Production plan** — this sets out **how many** products the business intends to produce, and how it will go about **producing** them (e.g. how many workers will be required, what the costs of production will be, etc.).

4) **Marketing plan** — the entrepreneur defines the **market** for the business and explains who its main **competitors** are, who the **target customers** are and what the product's **unique selling point** (see p.34) is. It includes details of any **market research** that the entrepreneur has done, and any **promotions** that they intend to run.

5) **Human resources plan** — outlines the relevant **qualifications** and **experience** of the entrepreneur and other people involved in setting up the business. It also sets out how many **employees** the business intends to take on, and how much it intends to pay them.

6) **Operations plan** — gives details of where the business will be **located**, whether the business will **own** or **rent** property and machinery, etc.

7) **Financial plan** — covers all of the financial **forecasts** for the business, e.g. how much **capital** they need to start the business, how they are going to **finance** the business, and their **break-even** calculations (see p. 32-33). It also includes a **cash flow forecast** (see p. 34-35) and an estimated **profit and loss account** and **balance sheet** (see p. 44-47) for the first year. The financial information explains how the business will **survive** in the start-up period.

Business Plans

It's **Difficult** to produce an **Accurate** business plan

1) Business plans are **never** 100% accurate because it's **impossible** for a business to get accurate information about costs, revenue, etc. **before** it has started trading.

2) Just because the business plan says that the business should be making a profit of £2000 a month doesn't mean that that's what will actually happen — there's no way of knowing for definite what will really happen, so there's always **risk** involved in setting up a business.

3) However, producing a thorough business plan **reduces** the risk of the business failing.

Entrepreneurs can get **Advice** on creating a business plan

If only Bryan had taken some professional advice before setting up his cruise business, it might have worked out a lot better.

1) The business plan is **really important**, so entrepreneurs need to get it right.

2) Entrepreneurs can get **free** help and advice on writing a business plan from a government organisation like Business Link, or from the manager or Small Business Advisor at their bank — they can give entrepreneurs sample business plans or CDs that guide you through the process of writing a business plan. Some **websites** also provide sample business plans free of charge, which entrepreneurs can adapt to their own business.

3) Entrepreneurs can also get expert guidance and advice from business consultants or accountants, but this is a more **expensive** option.

Established Businesses produce business plans too

1) Business plans are not just for new start-up businesses — it can sometimes be very useful for **established** businesses to write a new business plan.

2) If a business is planning to launch a **new product**, creating a new business plan can allow managers to see whether it's likely to be **profitable**. If not, they might decide not to go ahead with the launch.

3) A new business plan can also be useful if the business is planning to **expand** (e.g. if the owner of a successful restaurant decides to open another branch in a different town) especially since they might need to find external **finance** to do it.

Eilidh's clothes shop was a big success in Dundee, but she'd have saved a lot of money if she'd done a new business plan before she opened the branch in Chelmsford.

Practice Questions

Q1 What is usually the main reason for producing a business plan?

Q2 Why is the executive summary important?

Q3 Give five examples of information that's covered in a business plan.

Q4 Name three sources of expert advice on creating a business plan.

Exam Question

Q1 Explain why every new business should have a business plan. (10 marks)

"Slaps bunnies" and "painless buns" — anagrams of "business plan..."

Business plans are quite straightforward really — if you're going to open a business then it makes sense to plan what you're going to do. Just learn the main things that a business plan includes, and why entrepreneurs need to produce them, and remember that producing an accurate plan for a new business is always a bit of a problem.

Economic Influences

The economic climate has a big impact on businesses — falls in interest rates can be great news for businesses, but inflation and unemployment can be a big pain in the backside. **These pages are only for Edexcel.**

Interest Rates *significantly influence business*

1) The interest rate is the **reward** offered to savers and the **cost** of **borrowing** money.
    For example, if you borrow £100 and pay 5% interest a year, you'll be paying £5 interest a year.

2) **Higher interest rates** mean **less disposable income** (the income you have left after paying taxes, mortgage, etc.).
    This is because **most** people **borrow** the money to pay for things like mortgages, credit cards, loans and
    overdrafts rather than using their **savings**. Because people have less to spend, **demand falls**. High interest rates
    make the **cost of borrowing** higher and they make **savings** more **attractive** than spending, which also reduces
    demand. Because it costs more for businesses to borrow money, businesses suffer and **unemployment rises**.

3) **Lower interest rates** mean **more disposable income**. **Borrowing** is **cheaper**, and **saving** is **less attractive**. People
    can borrow money to spend, so **demand rises** and businesses **prosper**.

    Here's the **relationship** between interest rates, spending, demand and unemployment:

When the interest rate changes, it causes all the other factors shown in the table to change too.

Interest rates	Disposable income	Consumer spending	Demand in the economy	Economic output	Unemployment
go up ↑	goes down ↓	goes down ↓	goes down ↓	goes down ↓	goes up ↑
go down ↓	goes up ↑	goes up ↑	goes up ↑	goes up ↑	goes down ↓

4) The **effect** that interest rates have on **demand** depends on the particular product, and whether you're likely to
    need to **borrow money** to buy it. Demand for **new cars** is affected a lot — when interest rates are high, people
    keep their old car instead of taking out an **expensive loan** for a new one.

5) Firms' **investment** is also affected by interest rates. When interest rates are low, investment projects become
    more attractive and firms borrow money to invest in fixed assets.

Inflation — *Prices go* Up, *the* Value of Money *goes* Down...

1) Inflation is measured by the **Consumer Prices Index** (CPI) which lists the prices
    of hundreds of goods and services which the average household would buy.

2) There's always **some** inflation, but the government tries to keep it fairly low
    — recently it's been less than 3% a year.

The CPI includes mortgage interest payments. Taking out these payments gives the underlying rate of inflation. Leaving them in gives the headline rate of inflation.

3) High inflation can be caused by **high demand** in the economy — more than
    the economy can supply. This is called **demand-pull** inflation. Excess demand
    when the economy is near its full capacity is called **overheating**.

4) Rises in inflation can be caused by **rising costs** pushing up **prices** — this is called **cost-push** inflation.
    Wage rises can cause prices to go up — firms might have to put prices up to **cover** increased wage costs.

5) **Expectations** of inflation can make inflation worse. A firm that expects its **suppliers** to put their prices up might
    put its **own** prices up to cover increased costs. Employees' expectations of rising prices can make them demand
    higher wages, which makes prices go up. This is the **wage-price spiral** — it's a big cause of cost-push inflation.

6) Inflation can have **serious economic effects**. The faster and higher the inflation, the worse the effects are.

    - An **increase** in **inflation** can cause **spending** to go **up temporarily** — people **rush to buy more** before
      prices go up even more. But if wages don't go up in line with inflation, sales go down as people can
      afford less. Sales don't go down as much with **demand-pull** inflation — demand-pull inflation happens
      because there's high demand.

    - Inflation causes **uncertainty** and makes it hard for businesses to **plan ahead**. This makes them **invest less**.

    - Inflation can be **good for borrowing** money and **bad for lending** money — loans are worth more when
      you get them than they are when you have to repay them.

    - **Cost-push** inflation makes **profit margins** go **down** if businesses decide not to put up their prices.

    - **Demand-pull** inflation can actually make **profit margins** go **up**. Firms operating at or near full capacity
      (see p.62-63) can put up prices in response to **high demand** without their **costs** going up by as much.

    - Inflation in the UK makes UK **exports** expensive abroad, so UK businesses become **less competitive**.

7) The impact of inflation depends on **how high** inflation is, what's **causing** it and how high inflation is in
    other countries. Read exam questions about inflation carefully before you launch into an answer.

Economic Influences

Unemployment is a Waste of Labour Resources

1) There are two main types of unemployment:

> **Structural** unemployment is due to changes in the structure of the economy, e.g. a **decline** in a **major industry** like coal mining. Structural unemployment is often concentrated in particular regions of the country.

> **Cyclical** unemployment is due to a **downturn** in the business cycle, i.e. a lack of **demand** for labour.

2) High unemployment can affect **sales**. Producers of **luxury** goods are badly affected by cyclical unemployment. Businesses producing **essentials** aren't affected all that much.

3) **Structural** unemployment affects **local** businesses — unemployed people have little money to spend.

4) When unemployment is **high**, businesses can hire staff easily. There's a good **supply** of labour, so businesses won't have to pay **high wages**. People in work will be extra **productive** to protect their jobs.

5) If unemployment is **structural** or **regional**, it's not all that easy to hire staff. Unemployed workers often aren't in the **right place** or from the **right industry** for the jobs that are out there — they need **training**.

The Government's Economic Policy influences business

1) **Monetary policy** involves controlling the **money supply** (how much money is in circulation) and changing **interest rates**. UK interest rates are now controlled by the Bank of England, independently of the government.

2) **Fiscal policy** determines the levels of **taxation** and **government spending**. The government is completely in charge of fiscal policy.

3) Taxes can be **direct taxes** like income tax on **individual earnings** and corporation tax on **business profits**, or they can be **indirect taxes** on **spending**, for example **VAT** (Value Added Tax, which you pay on almost everything you buy).

4) Government spending includes spending on **benefits**, spending on **construction** projects and spending on **defence** and **law and order**. Government spending helps businesses — e.g. giving people higher welfare benefits means they'll **spend** more money in the economy, building a motorway creates jobs for **civil engineers** and **construction workers**, and ordering more fighter planes helps **defence firms** like BAE Systems.

5) If demand in the economy is too low, governments try to increase it. They **cut taxes** so people have more to spend, and **increase** their **spending** in the economy (by raising benefits, building new roads, etc.). Central banks (e.g. the Bank of England) **reduce interest rates** to cut mortgage payments and increase disposable income.

6) Governments try to **reduce demand** if it's too high. They **raise taxes** so people have less money to spend, and **cut government spending**. Central banks **increase interest rates** to raise the cost of borrowing, reduce disposable income and reduce demand.

Practice Questions

Q1 How does a rise in interest rates affect consumer spending?
Q2 What is inflation?
Q3 What are the two main types of unemployment?
Q4 Who sets interest rates in the UK?

Exam Questions

Q1 Describe two ways in which an increase in interest rates could affect a large manufacturing company. (10 marks)

Q2 Discuss the circumstances under which governments try to influence the economy, and the methods they use. (10 marks)

Is your interest rate holding up, or are you starting to get slightly bored...

Blimey. After all that I almost feel qualified enough to go on the Today programme and talk about why the Bank of England's been putting interest rates up. Notice I said "almost". I do feel qualified to write an essay about interest rates, inflation, unemployment and economic policy — which is a good thing, because that's exactly what this page is for.

Social Influences

As if businesses didn't already have enough to worry about, they've also got to deal with social and ethical issues.
This page is for OCR, but there's a bit at the bottom for WJEC.

Demographic Changes affect business

1) **Demographics** are the **characteristics** of populations — e.g. age, gender, level of income, marital status, socioeconomic class, and level of education.

2) Different **groups** of consumers (e.g. the retired, or young professionals) tend to buy different **products**, so demographic changes can have an impact on **what** businesses decide to **produce**, and how they **market** goods.

3) Demographic changes also affect **how** businesses are run and what kind of new businesses people decide to set up. In recent years, an increase in the number of **working mothers** means that there has been increased demand for **childcare**, so more nurseries and childcare businesses have been set up. Businesses are also **employing** more working mothers, so they have to **adapt** to this and offer things like flexible working hours.

4) **Immigration** is another example of demographic change — e.g. immigration from **Poland** into the **UK** has led to supermarkets like Tesco stocking Polish brands of food, because the demand for these brands has grown. The need for **Polish language** skills in businesses and public services like healthcare has increased due to the rise in native Polish speakers in the population, and Polish **employees** can fulfil this need.

Businesses have Social Responsibilities

1) **Social responsibilities** are things that a business owes to society. Recent **social trends** have affected firms' social responsibilities. These include **environmentalism**, concerns about **business ethics** and **animal rights**, and an increased interest in **health** and **fitness**.

2) Social awareness has prompted some firms to:

   - produce **environmental** and **social audits** — independent checks on the firm's impact on the environment and society.

   - get raw materials from **fair trade** sources, paying producers in Less Economically Developed Countries (LEDCs) a fair price so that they can earn decent wages.

   - change their **marketing** to emphasise **social responsibility**, e.g. the Co-op advertises the fact that all its chocolate is fair trade.

   - change their marketing to emphasise responsibility for **health**, e.g. marketing a food product as a healthy option, low in salt, sugar and saturated fat.

   Being socially responsible can be a good USP for marketing (see p.86).

3) Businesses might act in a socially responsible way because of consumer pressure, because they legally have to, or because the business owner cares about social issues.

Environmental issues can Affect Business Decisions

1) Current environmental issues include **global warming** and **acid rain** (which are related to emissions from road and air traffic), **energy consumption**, **recycling** and reducing **packaging**, and the disposal of **waste**.

2) Businesses can set **targets** to **reduce pollution**, increase their use of renewable energy sources, increase recycling and reduce packaging, use sustainable materials, etc.

3) The main **business advantage** of taking environmental issues seriously is a good, caring corporate image among consumers and investors. Businesses with a "green" reputation can attract **new customers** and **increased sales**.

4) The main disadvantage is higher **costs**. Green production is almost always quite a bit more expensive.

Social Enterprises are businesses with Social Motives

1) **Social enterprises** make a **profit**, but their main aim is to solve **social** or **environmental** problems. E.g. the **Big Issue** is a social enterprise — homeless people can buy the Big Issue magazine for 70p, and they sell it on the streets for £1.50, keeping the 80p profit. **Housing associations** are another example of a social enterprise — they provide affordable housing for people on low incomes.

2) **Worker cooperatives** are a type of social enterprise in which the **employees** of a company **own** and **control** the business themselves. Each employee owns **one share** in the company and is allowed **one vote** when decisions about the business are made. ── *WJEC* ──────────────────────────────── *WJEC* ──

WJEC

WJEC

Ethical Issues

This top part of this page is for OCR. The lower part is for OCR, AQA and WJEC.

Ethics are Moral Principles of Right and Wrong ──── OCR ────

1) Consumers seem to be more and more concerned about **business ethics** these days.

2) They worry about firms using **cheap labour** in LEDCs (Less Economically Developed Countries), especially **child labour** (some products are made abroad by kids as young as 8 years old). People worry that workers in LEDCs don't have as much protection against **exploitation** and poor working conditions as people in the UK.

3) Lots of consumers worry about **environmentally unfriendly products** and **animal testing** bothers some people.

4) Many people are also concerned about **obesity**, and think it's wrong for businesses to promote **unhealthy food**.

How businesses deal with ethical issues:

- Businesses may have an **ethical code** which sets out how they deal with **customers** and **suppliers**, their behaviour towards the **environment**, and how **employees** should behave.

- Acting **ethically** may increase or decrease a firm's profits. Actions which **attract customers** and **investors**, and help to **recruit** and retain **loyal** and **productive employees** all help to **increase profits**. Actions which **cost more** in raw materials, production methods and staff training **reduce profits**.

- Businesses often find it **hard** to implement ethical policies. Ethical policies can conflict with a firm's existing objectives, including the aim of high profits. Consumers may be **suspicious** of the firm's motives — they may think the firm is just trying to make itself **look** socially responsible to improve its **image**. Employees could **resist** changes to their working practices.

──── OCR ──────────── OCR ────

Competition between businesses can be Fair or Unfair

1) **Fair competition** (also called **perfect competition**) is where all businesses compete on an **equal** basis — they have to compete on **quality** and **price**, so consumers get products with the **best** quality and the **lowest** price.

2) A **monopoly** is where one business has **complete control** over its market. There's **no** competition. Since there are no alternatives, if the consumer **needs** the product, the monopoly business can charge whatever **price** it wants for it and consumers will be **forced** to pay that price. This is **good** for the business, because it can lead to huge profits, but can be very **unfair** to consumers. In the UK, the Competition Commission considers any business with over 25% of the market to be a monopoly, and can intervene to stop monopolies occurring.

3) **Monopolistic competition** is when businesses in the same market have a strong enough **brand** for competition in these circumstances to **not** be based just on price — consumers choose products based on **brand image**, so businesses **don't** have to keep their prices low if they've got a popular brand.

4) In an **oligopoly**, a **small** number of **large** firms dominate a market, and keep their prices at a **similar level**. If the consumer **needs** the product, they must pay this price. This means that the firms don't really compete over price, but have to focus more on marketing and brand image. This is **good** for the **businesses** because they can make bigger profits than they would in perfect competition, but **not** so good for the **consumers** who are forced to pay higher prices. It's still fair competition though — it's not the same as **price-fixing**, when businesses get together and **agree** to charge the same **high prices**. Examples of oligopolies in the UK are the supermarket trade or chocolate bars.

Practice Questions

Q1 Define "demographic changes".

Q2 Give two examples of recent social trends that have affected businesses.

Q3 Give the meanings of monopoly, oligopoly and fair competition.

Exam Question

Q1 A supermarket chain is considering ways of making its stores and products more environmentally friendly. Suggest what measures they might introduce and evaluate whether they would be beneficial to the firm. (10 marks)

This page is free of genetically modified organisms...

Being socially responsible costs money. Whether a business decides to make some ethical change to its policy usually depends on how much consumers want it to make that change. If they think that it'll encourage more consumers to buy their products then they'll do it — otherwise they probably won't bother.

Costs, Revenues and Profits

Businesses need to know how much their revenue and costs are — otherwise they wouldn't have a clue how much profit they were making. Costs, revenues and profits are all related.
These pages are for AQA, OCR, Edexcel and WJEC.

Revenue is the Money a business makes from Sales

1) Revenue is the **value of sales** — it's sometimes just called **sales**, and can also be called **turnover**. It's the amount of money generated by sales of a product, **before** any deductions are made.

2) You can work out the revenue by multiplying the **price** that the customer pays for each item by the **number of items** that the business sells.

> Revenue = selling price per item × quantity of items sold

Costs can be Fixed or Variable

1) **Fixed costs** don't change with output. **Rent** on a factory, business **rates**, **senior managers' salaries** and the cost of **new machinery** are fixed costs. When output increases, a business makes more use of the facilities it's got — the **cost** of those facilities **doesn't change**.

2) **Variable costs** rise and fall as output changes. Hourly **wages**, **raw materials** and **packaging costs** for each product are variable costs.

3) **Semi-variable** costs have fixed and variable parts. **Telephone bills** are good examples of **semi-variable** costs. Businesses have to pay a **fixed** amount for their phone line plus a **variable** amount depending on how many phone calls they've made.

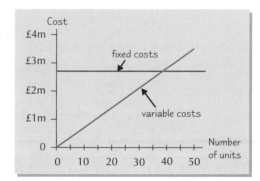

Costs can be Direct or Indirect ——————— OCR

1) **Direct costs** are directly linked to a product or service. The cost of raw materials and the hourly wages paid to factory workers making a product are direct costs.

2) **Indirect costs** can't be directly linked to only one product or service. They're also called **overheads**. Wages and salaries paid to people who **aren't directly involved** in making the product (e.g. senior managers, canteen workers) are indirect costs, as are business rates and rent.

3) **Direct** costs are almost always **variable** costs. **Indirect** costs are almost always **fixed** costs.
———— OCR ———————————————————— OCR ————

Large-scale Production helps keep costs Low

> There's more about this on p. 60. It's called "economies of scale".

The more a business produces, the **lower** the **cost per unit** produced. This is because the **fixed costs** are **shared out** between **more items**. The best way to show this is with an example:

1) Lecco make microwave ovens. The **fixed costs** of running Lecco are £200 000 per year. The **variable costs** of materials and labour are £15 per microwave.

2) If Lecco make **5000 microwaves a year**, the total production costs are... £200 000 + (£15 × 5000) = **£275 000**. The **cost per microwave** is £275 000 ÷ 5000 = **£55**.

3) If Lecco make **20 000 microwaves a year**, the total production costs are... £200 000 + (£15 × 20 000) = **£500 000**. The **cost per microwave** is £500 000 ÷ 20 000 = **£25**.

Profit = Revenue – Costs

1) When you deduct the costs from the revenue, what is left is the **profit**.

2) **Gross profit** is what you get when you subtract **variable** costs from revenue.

3) **Net profit** is what you get when you subtract **fixed and variable** costs from revenue.

4) **Revenue** and **profit** are affected by both **sales volume** and **price**. The amount of sales you lose by putting the price up varies — see **price elasticity of demand** on p. 92.

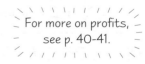

> For more on profits, see p. 40-41.

Costs, Revenues and Profits

Businesses use information on *Product Costs* to *Make Decisions*

1) Businesses use **cost** information to set the **selling price** of their products and services (see p.32). They set the price to make sure they'll make a **profit**. (Number of sales × price) – costs = profit.

2) If a business is a "**price-taker**" in a very competitive market, it **doesn't have control** of the **selling price** of its products — it takes whatever price the market will pay. Businesses in this situation need accurate **costing** information to work out if it's **profitable** to make and sell a product at all.

3) Businesses set **budgets** (see p. 36) which forecast how much costs are going to be over a year. Managers need to know what costs they're incurring **now**, so that they can know whether they're **meeting** the budget.

4) The **total costs** of making a product are the **fixed** costs and the **variable** costs added together. It can also be useful for a business to know the costs **per unit** of production — e.g. when making decisions about whether to increase or decrease output.

> For each unit, **costs = variable costs** + a **share** of the **fixed costs**

OCR — OCR — OCR — OCR — OCR — OCR

1) When a company **increases** or **decreases** output by **one unit**, it causes their **total** production **costs** to either **rise** or **fall**. This **change** in the **total cost** is known as the **marginal cost**.

2) In the **short-term**, increasing or decreasing output by one unit will only affect a company's **variable costs**. E.g a car production company will use fewer raw materials if it makes one less car, but it won't use fewer machines, so its fixed costs will not change. Because of this, **marginal cost** in the short term is a **variable** cost.

Costs also relate to *Missed Opportunities*

Two cars... or 30 holidays... or 8000 McDonald's Value Meals...

1) **Opportunity cost** puts a value on a product or business decision in terms of what the business had to give up to have it.

2) Businesses must **choose** where to spend their limited finance. Managers **compare opportunity costs** when making their decisions. The opportunity cost of an advert half way through an episode of X Factor might be five screenings of the same advert in the middle of Emmerdale.

Practice Questions

Q1 What is the formula for calculating revenue?

Q2 How is net profit calculated?

Q3 Give three examples of a fixed cost.

Q4 What is an opportunity cost?

Answer on p.108.

Exam Questions

Q1 Explain what is meant by the term 'variable costs', (2 marks)

Q2 Beth Brook Hats employs two hat-makers, each at £280/week. Beth, as Managing Director, pays herself £400/week. The other fixed costs are £300/week. The variable costs of raw materials are £14 per hat. Hats sell for £50.
(a) Draw a graph to show fixed, variable and total costs for outputs from 0 hats/week to 100 hats/week. (6 marks)
(b) Calculate the profit that Beth is making at her current output level of 60 hats per week, assuming weekly sales match output. (4 marks)

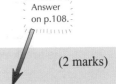

If you don't learn this, it'll cost you...

Costs, revenue and profit are kind of at the heart of this section. They're pretty simple concepts, but they're used to work out everything else, so make sure you get them straight in your head. You need to be able to calculate revenue and profit, so learn the formulas well, and make sure you're clear on the difference between fixed and variable costs too.

Break-Even Analysis

Break-even analysis is a great way of working out how much you need to sell to make profit.
This page is for AQA, OCR, Edexcel and WJEC.

Breaking Even means Covering your Costs

1) The **break-even point** is the level of sales a business needs to **cover their costs**. At this point, costs = revenue.

2) When sales are **below** the break-even point, costs are more than revenue — the business makes a **loss**. When sales are **above** the break-even point, revenue exceeds costs — the business makes a **profit**.

3) **New businesses** should always do a **break-even analysis** to **find** the break-even point. It tells them how much they will need to sell in order to break even. They need to decide whether the level of sales needed to break even is achievable — if not then it's probably a bad idea to launch the business. **Established businesses** use break-even analysis to decide whether or not to launch new products.

Contribution is used to work out the Break-Even Output

1) **Contribution** is the difference between the **selling price** of a product and the **variable costs** it takes to produce it.

> Contribution per unit = selling price per unit – variable costs per unit

If a business sells lots of different products, each one might have a different contribution.

2) Contribution is used to **pay fixed costs**. The amount left over is profit.

3) **The break-even point** is where **contribution = fixed costs**. **Break-even output** is fixed costs over contribution per unit.

$$\text{Break-even output} = \frac{\text{fixed costs}}{\text{contribution per unit}}$$

> **Example:** Harry sets up a business to print T-shirts. The **fixed costs** of premises and the T-shirt printers are **£3000**. The **variable costs** per T-shirt (the T-shirt, ink, wages) are **£5**. Each printed T-shirt sells for **£25**.
>
> **Contribution per unit** = £25 – £5 = **£20**   **Break-even output** = £3000 ÷ £20 = **150**
> So, Harry has to sell **150** T-shirts to **break even**.
>
> The **revenue** at the break-even output is the **break-even revenue** — break-even revenue is 150 x £25 = **£3750**.

Draw a Break-Even Chart to show the Break-Even Point

1) Break-even charts show **costs** and **revenues** plotted against **output**. Businesses use break-even charts to see how costs and revenues **vary** with different levels of output.

2) **Output** goes on the **horizontal axis**. The scale needs to let you plot output from 0 to the maximum possible.

3) **Costs and revenue** both go on the vertical axis. Use a scale that lets you plot from 0 to the maximum revenue.

4) Plot **fixed** costs. (On the diagram on the right, fixed costs are the blue horizontal line.)

5) **Add** variable costs to fixed costs to get the **total cost**, and plot it on the graph. (The total costs are shown by the purple line, starting at the same point as the fixed costs line.)

6) Next, plot **revenue** on the graph. (It's the green line on the diagram.)

7) The **break-even point** is where the **revenue** line crosses the **total costs** line.

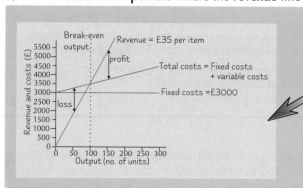

Changing either the **variable costs** or the **price** of the products will affect the break-even point.

Looking at how the break-even point changes when other factors change is called "what-if analysis".

This graph shows that if Harry **increased the price** of the T-shirts to £35 each, his break-even output would be **lowered** to 100 units. You could also work this out using the formula for break-even output:

Contribution per unit = £35 – £5 = **£30**
Break-even output = £3000 ÷ £30 = **100**

Break-Even Analysis

The **Margin of Safety** is the amount between **Current Output** and **Break Even**

Margin of safety = current output − break-even output

1) OK, back to Harry's T-shirt business again. The diagram on the right shows the margin of safety for Harry's business when his output is 250 T-shirts. If Harry sells **250** T-shirts, the margin of safety is 250 − 150 = **100**. He can sell up to 100 fewer T-shirts before he starts to lose money.

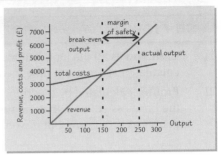

2) If his output changed to **300** T-shirts, the margin of safety would go up to 300 − 150 = **150**.

3) Knowing the break-even point and margin of safety allows businesses to make **important decisions** — if Harry's calculations show that his T-shirt business has a low margin of safety, he can take action to increase it by either **lowering his costs** or **increasing his revenue**.

4) This would **lower** his break-even point, so he'd have a **greater** margin of safety. A big margin of safety is useful for a business because it means less risk.

Remember that changing costs or revenue will also have an effect on profits.

Break-Even Analysis has **Advantages** and **Disadvantages**

Advantages of break-even analysis	Disadvantages of break-even analysis
It's **easy** to do. If you can plot figures on a graph accurately, you can do break-even analysis.	Break-even analysis assumes that **variable costs** always rise steadily. This isn't always the case — a business can get **discounts** for buying in bulk so costs don't go up in **direct proportion** to output.
It's **quick** — managers can see the **break-even point** and **margin of safety** immediately so they can take **quick action** to cut costs or increase sales if they need to **increase** their margin of safety.	Break-even analysis is simple for a **single product** — but most businesses sell lots of different products, so looking at the business as a whole can get a lot more complicated.
Break-even charts let businesses **forecast** how variations in sales will affect **costs**, **revenue** and **profits** and, most importantly, how variations in **price** and **costs** will affect how **much** they **need** to **sell**.	If the **data** is wrong, then the **results** will be wrong.
Businesses can use break-even analysis to help **persuade** the bank to give them a **loan**.	Break-even analysis assumes the business sells **all the products**, without any wastage. But, for example, a restaurant business will end up throwing away food if fewer customers turn up than they're expecting.
Break-even analysis influences decisions on whether **new products** are launched or not — if the business would need to sell an unrealistic volume of products to break even, they would probably decide **not** to launch the product.	Break-even analysis only tells you how many units you **need** to sell to break even. It doesn't tell you how many you're **actually going to sell**.

Practice Questions

Q1   Write down the formula for contribution, and the formula for break-even output.

Q2   Write down two advantages and two disadvantages of break-even analysis.

Answer on p. 108.

Exam Questions

Q1   Bob is deciding whether to set up in business selling fishing equipment. Evaluate the value of break-even analysis in helping Bob decide whether or not to go ahead with the business.   (10 marks)

Q2   Muneer Khan has a small restaurant. The average price per customer per meal is £13. The variable costs of materials and labour per meal are £5. The fixed costs of the restaurant are £1000 per month. Calculate the break-even number of customers per month.   (4 marks)

Ah, give us a break...

You might be asked to calculate the break-even point or draw it on a graph, so make sure you can do both. Make sure you can also give examples of how the break-even point is used by businesses to make decisions, and learn some advantages and disadvantages of break-even analysis. Then give yourself a pat on the back and move on to the next page.

Cash Flow Forecasting

Cash flow is money flowing in and out of a business. It's vital to have enough money to meet your immediate debts — otherwise the people you owe money to start getting cross. **These pages are for AQA, OCR, Edexcel and WJEC.**

Cash Flow isn't the same as Profit

1) **Cash flow** is all the money flowing **into** and **out of** the business over a period of time, calculated at the **exact time** the cash **enters** or **leaves** the bank account or till.

2) **Profit** is calculated by recording all transactions that will **lead** to cash going **in** or **out** of the business either at that moment or at some point in the **future**. Selling something on credit counts as profit now, but it won't count as cash flow until the customer actually pays for it.

The Cash Flow Cycle is the Gap between Money Going Out and Coming In

1) Businesses need to **pay money out** for fixed assets (e.g. buildings, machinery and vehicles) and operating costs to fulfil an order **before** they **get paid** for that order. New businesses **need money** to spend on start-up costs **before** they've even started to get any sales at all.

2) This **delay** between money going out and money coming in is the **cash flow cycle** — as in the diagram.

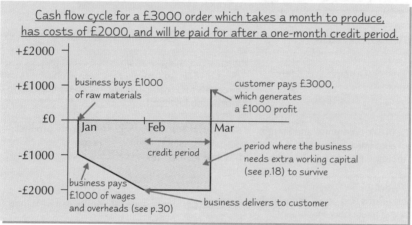

Cash flow cycle for a £3000 order which takes a month to produce, has costs of £2000, and will be paid for after a one-month credit period.

\ \ \ \ | | / / / /
Bankruptcy is for sole
traders/partnerships,
and insolvency is
for companies.
/ / / | | \ \ \ \

3) It's important to make sure there's always **enough money** available to pay **suppliers** and **wages**. Not paying suppliers and employees can be something of a **disaster**.

4) If a business **produces too much**, they'll have to **pay** suppliers and staff **so much** that they'll go **bankrupt** or **insolvent** before they have the chance to **get paid** by their customers. This is called **overtrading**.

5) **Cash flow calculations** are pretty much **the most important thing** to a business in the **short term**. Businesses need cash to survive. Looking at the **long term**, **profit** is important — making profit is the main objective for businesses.

Businesses have Various Canny Tricks to Improve cash flow

1) Businesses try to **reduce the time** between **paying** suppliers and **getting money** from customers. They try to get their **suppliers** to give them a **longer** credit period — and give their **customers** a **shorter** credit period. It's important to **balance** the need to manage cash flow with the need to keep suppliers and customers **happy** — you don't want customers to go elsewhere.

2) Businesses can try to hold less **stock**, so less cash is tied up in stock.

3) **Credit controllers** keep **debtors** in control. They set credit limits and remind debtors to pay up.

4) **Debt factoring** gives instant cash to businesses whose customers haven't paid their invoices. Banks and other financial institutions act as **debt factoring agents**. The agent pays the business about **80%** of the value of the invoice as an **instant cash advance**. The agent gets the customer to pay up, and then **keeps** about **5%** of the value of the invoice — debt factoring costs money and the agent has to make a living.

5) **Sale and leaseback** is when businesses **sell** equipment to **raise capital**, and then **lease** (rent) the equipment back. That way, they get a big **lump sum** from the sale, and pay a **little** bit of money each month for the lease of the equipment. Of course, they don't get to own the equipment again unless they get enough cash to buy it back — and they have to pay the lease in the meantime.

Cash Flow Forecasting

Businesses make Cash Flow Forecasts to help them make decisions

1) **Cash flow forecasts** (also called cash budgets) show the amount of money that managers **expect** to **come into** and **flow out** of the business on a monthly basis over a period of time in the **future**.

2) Managers can use cash flow forecasts to **make sure** they always have **enough** cash around to pay **suppliers** and **employees**. They can **predict** when they'll be **short of cash**, and arrange a **loan** or **overdraft** in time.

3) Businesses show cash flow forecasts to **banks** and venture capitalists when trying to get **loans** and other finance. Cash flow forecasts prove that the business has an idea of where it's going to be in the future.

4) **Established** businesses tend to base their forecast on **past experience**. **New** companies don't have any past data, so their forecast needs to consider the business' **capacity**, experiences of **similar businesses** and trends in customer behaviour that have shown up in **market research**.

Here's how to Construct and Interpret a Cash Flow Forecast

Example: A new business starts up with a loan of £18 000 and £5000 of capital. It expects to sell £5000 worth of products in January, £35 000 in February, £35 000 in March and £40 000 in April. All customers will be granted a **one month credit period**. Wages and rent will cost £15 000 each month, and other costs are expected to be £5000 in January, £8000 in February, £2000 in March and £2000 in April.

This shows cash coming in from <u>sales</u> and from the initial <u>start-up loan</u>.

This shows <u>cash going out</u> to pay for the firm's <u>costs</u>.

<u>Net cash flow = total cash in – total costs</u>

	Item	Jan	Feb	Mar	Apr
Cash in	Sales revenue		£5000	£35000	£35000
	Other cash in	£18000			
	Total cash in	**£18000**	**£5000**	**£35000**	**£35000**
Cash out	Wages and rent	£15000	£15000	£15000	£15000
	Advertising/other costs	£5000	£8000	£2000	£2000
	Total costs	**£20000**	**£23000**	**£17000**	**£17000**
Net monthly cash flow	**Net cash flow**	**(£2000)**	**(£18000)**	**£18000**	**£18000**
	Opening balance	£5000	£3000	(£15000)	£3000
	Closing balance	**£3000**	**(£15000)**	**£3000**	**£21000**

April's sales revenue isn't included because it won't be paid until May, by the way.

Figures in brackets are <u>negative</u>.

According to this, the business will have £21 000 in the bank by the end of April. <u>But</u> it'll still owe £18 000 from the start-up loan ...

The <u>opening balance</u> is money in the bank at the start, in this case £5000.

<u>Closing balance = opening balance + net cash flow</u>

The <u>closing</u> balance for <u>last month</u> is <u>this month's opening balance</u>.

In the exam, you could be asked to fill in missing figures in a cash flow forecast, or even draw one from scratch.

Cash Flow Forecasting isn't always accurate

1) Cash flow forecasts can be based on **false assumptions** about what's going to happen.

2) Circumstances can **change suddenly** after the forecast's been made. **Costs** can **go up**. Machinery can **break down** and need mending. **Competitors** can put their prices up or down, which **affects sales**.

3) Good cash flow forecasting needs lots of **experience** and lots of **research** into the market.

4) A **false forecast** can have **disastrous** results. A business that runs out of cash can go **bankrupt** or **insolvent**.

Practice Questions

Q1 What's the difference between profit and cash flow?

Q2 Give two reasons why a cash flow forecast is useful to someone setting up their own small business.

Q3 If a company has total cash in of £8000 and total costs of £9500, what is its net cash flow?

Q4 If a company has an opening balance of £20000 and its net cash flow is (£7000), what is the closing balance?

Q5 How can you work out a company's opening balance in any given month?

Answers on p. 108.

Exam Questions

Q1 Examine the ways in which a business can improve its cash flow. (9 marks)

Q2 To what extent can a business successfully and accurately predict future cash flow? Explain your answer. (12 marks)

Dunno 'bout you, but cash flows through my wallet like water...

Cash flow is vitally important for a business — without it, businesses can go bankrupt or insolvent. Make sure you understand how to calculate the figures in the table on this page. It can be slightly tricky to start with, so go over it a few times until you really get it. Don't forget to learn the ways that businesses can improve their cash flow too.

Setting Budgets

Businesses make financial plans. They set targets for how much money they're going to make, and how much they're going to spend. Then they check to see how they've done, which sounds simple enough... **For all exam boards.**

A **Budget** is a **Financial Plan** for the future

A **budget** forecasts **future earnings** and **future spending**, usually over a 12 month period.
Businesses use different budgets to estimate different things. There are three types of budget:

1) **Income budgets** forecast the amount of money that will come into the company as revenue. In order to do this, the company needs to predict **how much** it will sell (see p.37), and at what **price**. Managers estimate this using their **sales figures** from previous years, as well as **market research.**

2) **Expenditure budgets** predict what the **total costs** will be for the year, taking into account both fixed and variable costs. Since variable costs increase with output, managers need to predict what the output will be (based on how much they expect to sell).

3) The **profit budget** uses the totals from the income and expenditure budgets to calculate what the expected **profit** (or **loss**) will be for that year.

Budgets affect **All Areas** of the business

1) The expenditure budget forecasts **total** expenditure. This is broken down into **department** (dept.) expenditure budgets — each department is allotted a certain amount of money to spend.

2) Department expenditure budgets are broken down into budgets for **specific activities** within the dept.

3) **Budget holders** are people **responsible** for spending or generating the money for each budget. For example, the budget holder of the expenditure budget for marketing would be the head of the marketing department.

4) The **master budgets** help businesses understand their cash flow situation **as a whole**, and the department and activity budgets help local managers control and coordinate their work.

5) Budgets **set targets** that can be used to **control** or **motivate** staff, depending on management style.

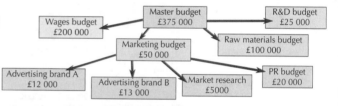

The **Budget Setting** process involves **Research** and **Negotiation**

1) To set the **income budget**, businesses **research** and **predict** how sales are going to go up and down through the year, so that they can make a good prediction of **sales revenue**.

2) To set the **expenditure budget** for **production**, businesses research how labour costs, raw materials costs, taxes and inflation are going to go up over the year. They can then figure out the **costs** of producing the volume of product that they think they're going to sell.

3) Annual budgets are usually agreed by **negotiation** — when budget holders have a say in setting their budgets, they're **motivated** to achieve them.

4) Budgets should **stretch** the abilities of the business, but they must be **achievable**. **Unrealistically** high income budgets or low expenditure budgets will **demotivate** staff. No one likes being asked to do the **impossible**.

5) Once they've agreed the budget, budget holders **keep checking** performance against the budget. This is called **variance analysis**. There's more about variance and variance analysis on p. 38-39.

Budgets have **Advantages** and **Disadvantages**

Benefits of budgeting

- Budgets help **control** income and expenditure. They show where the money goes.
- Budgeting forces managers to **review** their activities.
- Budgets let heads of department **delegate** authority to budget holders. Getting authority is **motivating**.
- Budgets allow departments to **coordinate** spending.
- Budgets help managers either **control** or **motivate** staff. Meeting a budget target is **satisfying**.

Drawbacks of budgeting

- Budgeting can cause **resentment** and rivalry if departments have to compete for money.
- Budgets can be **restrictive**. Fixed budgets stop firms responding to changing market conditions.
- Budgeting is **time-consuming**. Managers can get too preoccupied with setting and reviewing budgets, and forget to focus on the real issues of **winning business** and **understanding** the **customer**.

Setting Budgets

Businesses use **Sales Forecasting** to **Predict** how much they will **Sell**

1) Most businesses **forecast** sales **using** the **previous** year or quarter's **sales figures**, using both **internal** data (which shows the company's sales figures) and **external** data (which shows the figures for the industry as a whole.

2) **New businesses** don't have any internal data. They can forecast sales using **industry data**, the **opinions** of their **sales team** or by doing **test marketing** (see p.82) or by **researching** the **needs** of potential **customers**.

3) Both new and existing firms **often** get sales forecasts **wrong**. The number of sales can be affected by **social factors** (e.g. changes in fashion), **economic factors** (e.g a change in interest rates) or **technological developments.**

Budgets can be **Updated Every Year** or developed from **Scratch**

1) **Start-up businesses** have to develop their budgets **from scratch** (known as **zero budgeting**). This is difficult to do because they don't have much information to base their decisions on — they can't take into account the previous year's sales or expenditure. This means that their budgets are likely to be **inaccurate**.

2) After the first year, a business decides whether it wants to use **historical budgeting**, or stick with **zero budgeting**.

Historical budgets are updated each year

1) This year's budget is based on a percentage increase or decrease from last year's budget. For example, a firm expecting 10% revenue growth might add 10% to the advertising, wages and raw materials purchasing budgets.

2) Historical budgeting is **quick** and **simple** but it assumes that business conditions stay **unchanged** each year. This isn't always the case — for instance, a product at the introduction stage of its **life cycle** needs more money spent on advertising than one in the growth or maturity stages.

Zero budgeting means starting from scratch each year

1) Budget holders **start** with a budget of **£0**, and have to **bid** (or beg) for money to spend on activities.

2) They have to **plan** all the year's activities, ask for money to spend on them, and be prepared to **justify** their requests to the finance director. Budget holders need good negotiating skills for this.

3) Zero budgeting takes much **longer** to complete than historical budgeting.

4) If zero budgeting is done properly it's **more accurate** than historical budgeting.

5) This method is always used in **start-up businesses**.

Fixed Budgets can make businesses Inflexible

1) **Fixed budgets** provide **discipline** and **certainty**. This is especially important for a business with **liquidity** problems — fixed budgets help control **cash flow**.

2) **Fixed budgeting** means budget holders have to stick to their budget plans throughout the year. Fixed budgets can **prevent** a firm reacting to **opportunities** or **threats** that they didn't know about when they set the budget.

3) **Flexible budgeting** allows for budgets to be altered in response to significant changes in the market or economy.

4) **Zero budgeting** gives a business more **flexibility** than **historical budgeting**.

Practice Questions

Q1 Name the three main types of budget that a business will set, stating what each tells you.

Q2 If a business has an income budget of £125 000 and a profit budget of £30 000, what is its expenditure budget?

Q3 Explain the difference between fixed and flexible budgets.

Answer on p. 108.

Exam Questions

Q1 To what extent might fixed budgets help a manufacturer in the fast-changing computer software sector? (15 marks)

Q2 (a) Discuss the benefits that setting a budget will have for a new business. (6 marks)
(b) Discuss the problems that a new business might have in setting budgets for the first time. (9 marks)

I set myself a word budget today and I'm just about to run out...

Budgets are multi-purpose — as well as helping businesses forecast their future spending, they can motivate people, too. Luckily, you're not going to get marked on how good you are at budgeting in the exam — just on how well you understand what income, expenditure and profit budgets are, why businesses use them and how they set them.

Using Budgets

Variance is the difference between actual and budgeted spend. Managers look at variances to help them understand and control business performance. **These pages are for AQA, OCR, Edexcel and WJEC.**

Variance is the Difference between Actual figures and Budget figures

1) A variance means the business is performing either **worse** or **better** than expected.

2) A **favourable variance** leads to **profits increasing**. If revenue's more than the budget says it's going to be, that's a favourable variance. If costs are below the cost predictions in the budget, that's a favourable variance.

3) An **adverse variance** is a difference that **reduces profits**. Selling fewer items than the income budget predicts or spending more on an advert than the expenditure budget for marketing allows is an adverse variance.

4) Variances **add up**. For example, if actual sales exceed budgeted sales by £3000 and expenditure on raw materials is £2000 below budget, the variance is £3000 + £2000 = £5000, so there's a combined **favourable variance of** £5000.

5) If £10 000 is spent on raw materials in a month when the budget was only £6000, the variance is £6000 – £10000 = –£4000, so there is a £4000 **adverse variance.**

	Jan Budget	Jan Actual	Jan Variance	Feb Budget	Feb Actual	Feb Variance	Cumulative Variance
Revenue	£100k	£90k	£100k – £90k = £10k £10k (A)	£110k	£110k	£110k – £110k = £0 £0	–£10k + £0 = –£10k £10k (A)
Wages	£40k	£30k	£40k – £30k = £10k £10k (F)	£40k	£41k	£40k – £41k = –£1k £1k (A)	£10k –£1k = £9k £9k (F)
Rent	£10k	£10k	£10k – £10k = £0 £0	£10k	£11k	£10k – £11k = –£1k £1k (A)	£0 –£1k = –£1k £1k (A)
Other costs	£5k	£6k	£5k – £6k = –£1k £1k (A)	£5k	£6k	£5k – £6k = –£1k £1k (A)	–£1k + –£1k = –£2k £2k (A)
Total costs	£55k	£46k	£55k – £46k = £9k £9k (F)	£55k	£58k	£55k – £58k = –£3k £3k (A)	£9k –£3k = £6k £6k (F)

Variances can be calculated for each budget each month, for each budget as a running total, and for groups of budgets as a monthly or running total variance.

(A) means an adverse variance.
(F) means a favourable variance.

Variances can be Bad — even when they say you're doing Better than Expected

1) When variances occur, it means that what has happened is **not** what the business was expecting. Businesses need to know about variances so that they can find out **why** they have occurred.

2) It's extremely important to spot adverse variances as **soon** as possible. It's important to find out which budget holder is responsible — and to take action to fix the problem.

3) It's **also** important to **investigate favourable variances**. Favourable variances may mean that the budget targets weren't **stretching** enough — so the business needs to set more **difficult targets**.
The business also needs to understand **why** the performance is better than expected — if the department is **doing something right**, the business can **spread** this throughout the organisation.

Variances are caused by several factors — Internal and External

External Factors Cause Variance

1) **Competitor behaviour** and changing **fashions** may increase or reduce **demand** for products.
2) Changes in the **economy** can change how much workers' wages cost the business.
3) The cost of **raw materials** can go up — e.g. if a harvest fails.

Internal Factors Cause Variance

1) Improving **efficiency** (e.g. by introducing automated production equipment) causes **favourable** variances.
2) A business might **overestimate** the amount of money it can save by streamlining its production methods.
3) A business might **underestimate** the **cost** of making a change to its organisation.
4) Changing the selling price changes sales revenue — this creates variance if it happens after the budget's been set.
5) Internal causes of variance are a **serious concern**. They suggest that internal **communication** needs improvement.

Using Budgets

Variance Analysis means Identifying and Explaining variances

1) Variance analysis means **spotting** variances and figuring out **why** they've happened, so that action can be taken to fix them.

2) **Small** variances aren't a big problem. They can actually help to **motivate** employees. Staff try to **catch up** and sort out small **adverse** variances themselves. Small **favourable** variances can motivate staff to **keep on** doing whatever they were doing to create a favourable variance.

3) **Large** variances can **demotivate**. Staff don't work hard if there are large favourable variances — they **don't see the need**. Staff can get demotivated by a large **adverse** variance — they may feel that the task is **impossible**, or that they've **already failed**.

Businesses have to Do Something about variances

When variances occur, businesses can either change what the **business** is doing to make it fit the budget, or change the **budget** to make it fit what the **business** is doing. There are three factors that they need to take into account to make this decision:

1) Businesses need to **beware** of chopping and changing the budget **too much**.

2) Changing the budget **removes certainty** — which removes one of the big benefits of budgets.

3) Altering budgets can also make them **less motivating** — when staff start to expect that management will change targets instead of doing something to change performance, they don't see the point in trying any more.

Businesses Try to Fix Adverse Variances

1) They can change the **marketing mix** (see p.85). **Cutting prices** will increase sales — but only if the demand is price elastic (see p.92). **Updating** the product might make it more attractive to customers. Businesses can also look for a **new market** for the product, or change the **promotional strategy** — e.g. by advertising the product more or doing point of sales promotion.

2) **Streamlining production** makes the business more **efficient**, so this reduces costs.

3) They can try to motivate **employees** to **work harder**.

4) Businesses can try to cut costs by asking their **suppliers** for a **better deal**.

Businesses Try to Fix Favourable Variances

1) If the favourable variance is caused by a **pessimistic** budget, they make sure that they set more **ambitious targets** next time.

2) If the variance is because of **increased productivity** in one part of the business, they try to get everyone else doing whatever was **responsible** for the improvement.

Practice Questions

Q1 Define variance.

Q2 If a business sets an expenditure budget of £15 000 for marketing, and the actual expenditure for marketing is £18 000, how much is the variance and what type of variance is it?

Q3 Why are variances a concern for businesses?

Q4 State two external factors and two internal factors that cause variance.

Q5 How do businesses deal with variances?

Exam Question

Q1 (a) Using the figures in the table on p.38, calculate monthly and cumulative variances for March. Assume all budgets remain the same as February, and that actual sales are £120k, wages are £39k, rent is £11k, other costs are £5k and total costs are £55k. (8 marks)

(b) Explain what your answer to (a) suggests about the budget planning process for this company. (6 marks)

Answers on p.108.

Variance is one of those words that looks odd if you stare at it enough...

Variance variance variance variance variance... ahem... anyway. As well as knowing what businesses do when they set a budget, you need to know what they do when the real-life results don't quite match up to the budget prescriptions. Do they panic like you or I probably would — nope. They sort things out and get them shipshape again.

Measuring and Increasing Profit

Businesses need to measure their profit to find out how successful (or unsuccessful) they are.
These pages are for AQA, Edexcel and WJEC.

Profit is not the same as Revenue

1) **Revenue** is the amount of money that a business receives from sales of its products (see p. 30).
   But they **don't keep** all of it — the business also has **costs**.

2) When the business' **costs** are deducted from its **revenue**, what is left is the **profit**.

3) If the business' **costs** are **greater** than its **revenue**, it will make a **loss** instead of a profit.

Businesses want to Increase their profits

1) Most businesses exist to make a **profit** — if a business makes large profits then it is **successful**.
   Even successful businesses want to **increase profits** and become **more successful**.

2) Businesses can **improve** their **profits** by increasing their **prices** (if the demand for their products is price inelastic — see p.92) or **reducing** their prices to increase **demand** (if demand is price elastic). They could also try to reduce their **fixed costs** by changing utility provider or looking for a cheaper source of raw materials, decrease spending on **research and development** or use **marketing** to increase demand so that they sell more and make bigger profits.

3) Businesses **measure** their profits on a regular basis. They **compare** their profits from the current period (usually a year) to the profits from previous periods to measure their **progress**.

4) If profits go **down**, it's **bad news**, even if the business is still making large profits. E.g. if a firm makes £100 million of profit in a year, it might seem like good news, but if the previous year's profits were £125 million, it's a **bad sign**.

5) This is why businesses work out the **percentage increase** or **decrease** in their profits from year to year — it makes it easy to see how well they're performing in comparison with other years.

6) If profits are decreasing, the firm needs to investigate **why** this is happening and **take action** to resolve the issue.

The formula for measuring the **percentage change** in profit is:

> In the exam, set your workings out like the formula.

$$\text{Percentage Change in Profit} = \frac{\text{Current Year's Profit} - \text{Previous Year's Profit}}{\text{Previous Year's Profit}} \times 100\%$$

If a business makes a profit of **£20 000** in one year and **£30 000** the next year, the percentage change in profit is (£30 000 – £20 000) ÷ £20 000 × 100 = 50% — a **50% rise** in profits.

If a business makes a profit of **£10 000** in a year after having made a profit of **£15 000** in the previous year, the percentage change in profit is (£10 000 – £15 000) ÷ £15 000 × 100 = –33% — a **fall** in profits of **33%**.

There are Two Types of profit — Gross Profit and Net Profit

1) **Gross profit** is the amount left over when the **cost of making the products** is taken away.
   You can calculate **gross profit** by subtracting **variable costs** from the **revenue**.

> **Gross Profit = Revenue – Variable Costs**

2) **Net profit** takes into consideration not only the cost of actually producing each product, but also the **fixed costs** involved in running the business (for more on fixed and variable costs, see p. 30).
   You get the **net profit** by subtracting both **fixed costs** and **variable costs** from the **revenue**.

> **Net Profit = Revenue – (Fixed Costs + Variable Costs)**

Polly hoped that her net profit would increase enough for her to be able to make a whole dress.

Example

Hannah's Hammers is a small company selling hammers with a floral design.
The variable cost of producing each hammer is **£2**, and they are sold for **£5** each.
Hannah also has fixed costs of **£15 000** a year.

If Hannah sells **10 000** hammers in a year, her **revenue** is 10 000 × £5 = **£50 000**.

Hannah's **gross profit** is £50 000 – (£2 x 10 000) = **£30 000**.

Her **net profit** is £50 000 – (£15 000 + £20 000) = **£15 000**.

Measuring and Increasing Profit

Net Profit Margins show how Profitable a business or product is

1) Net profit margins measure the relationship between the **net profits made** and the **volume of sales**. They tell you what **percentage** of the selling price of a product is actually **net profit**.

2) Businesses can calculate their profit margins for **individual products**, or for the company **as a whole**.

3) The net profit margin is expressed as a percentage — the formula is:

$$\text{Net Profit Margin} = \frac{\text{Net Profit}}{\text{Revenue}} \times 100\%$$

4) It's best to have a **high** net profit margin, although it does depend on the type of business.

5) The net profit margin can be improved by **raising prices** or **lowering the cost of making the products** or (most importantly) the **fixed costs**. Raising prices might cause **demand** to **fall** though (see price elasticity of demand, p. 92,) so **increasing** the net profit **margin** too much could end up having a **negative** effect on **profits**. Similarly, **reducing** the **cost** of making the products could be **risky** if it affects the level of **quality**.

6) A business can improve its overall net profit margin if it **stops** selling products with a **low net profit margin**.

7) If a business has a revenue of £60 000 and a net profit of £18 000, its net profit margin is (£18 000 ÷ £60 000) × 100% = **30%**.

8) If the business manages to reduce its fixed costs the following year by £3000, and turnover stays the same, the new net profit will be £21 000, so the net profit margin will rise to (£21 000 ÷ £60 000) × 100 = **35%**.

Return on Capital Employed (ROCE) is an Important Profitability Ratio

1) The **return on capital employed** (ROCE) is considered to be the **best** way of analysing **profitability**.

2) The **ROCE** tells you how much money is **made** by the business, compared to how much money's been **put into** the business. It tells you how good the business is at generating profits from money invested.

3) In order to calculate the ROCE, you need to know what the **net profit** is, **excluding** any profit made from **one-off activities** (e.g. if a carpet-cleaning business raises £700 by putting on a raffle, this **shouldn't** be included in the ROCE calculation).

4) You also need to know the figure for **capital employed**. Capital employed means all the money that has been **invested** in the business, so it refers to the money that has come into the business from **loans** and **shares**.

5) ROCE is expressed as a percentage — the formula for calculating it is:

$$\text{Return on Capital Employed} = \frac{\text{Net Profit}}{\text{Capital Employed}} \times 100\%$$

6) A good **ROCE** is about **20%**, but 10-15% is OK. It's important to compare the ROCE with the Bank of England interest rate at the time — if the return is less than the interest rate then the investors would have been better off putting their money in the bank.

7) A business can improve its ROCE by using part of its net profit to **pay off some debts** — this will reduce capital employed. Another way to improve the ROCE is by making the business more **efficient** to **increase net profit**.

not Edexcel

Practice Questions

Q1 If a business makes a profit of £50 000 in 2006 and £52 000 in 2007, what is the percentage change in profit?

Q2 What is the formula for calculating Return on Capital Employed?

Q3 Give two ways in which Return on Capital Employed can be improved.

Exam Questions

Q1 Calculate the ROCE for a business with a net profit of £100 000 and capital employed of £40 000. (2 marks)

Q2 A business has a revenue of £2 million. Its gross profit is £750 000, and its fixed costs are £250 000.
(a) Calculate the net profit margin. (4 marks)
(b) Recommend what the business could do to improve the net profit margin. Explain why you're making this recommendation. (6 marks)

Answers on p. 108.

I'm just about 100% fed up with all these percentage calculations...

OK, I admit this hasn't been the world's most interesting page but this is all really important stuff, so make sure you get your head around it before moving on. You need to be able to calculate net profit margin and ROCE, so learn the formulas — you also need to understand what they actually mean for a business, and how businesses can improve their profitability.

Investment Decisions

Investment appraisal helps businesses decide what projects to invest in, to get the best, fastest, least risky return on their money. Sounds like a job for a guy with red braces to me. **These pages are for OCR only.**

Investment decisions must balance Risk and Return

1) Any situation where you need to **spend money** in order to **make money** is investment. **Investment** can mean buying shares in a business (**external investment**). It can also be **internal investment** — e.g. buying a large **asset,** spending money on **promotion**, **expanding** into an overseas market, reorganising, or developing a **new brand**.

> Money used to buy **fixed assets** is called **capital expenditure** — capital expenditure is an **investment** and allows the business to grow. **Revenue expenditure** is used to pay for the daily running of the business — it's money that's **gone** for good.

2) Any situation where you have to spend money in order to make money has **risk**.

3) Investors like the **risks** to be **low** and the **return** (profit) to be **high**. If circumstances are good, businesses can take more risks with investments, but in **uncertain** circumstances, they need to make sure that the risk is **low**.

4) There are a number of **investment appraisal tools** used to weigh up the **risk** and **reward** of the available projects. All of these methods are useful, but they're only as good as the **data** used to calculate them.

5) Investment appraisal methods assess how much **profit** a project is going to make, and how **fast** the money will come in. The faster money comes in, the less risk in the long run.

Payback measures the Length of Time it takes to Get Your Money Back

1) The **payback period** is the time it takes for the project to make enough money to pay back the initial investment.

2) For example, a £2 million project that has an annual profit prediction of £250 000 will reach payback in 8 years (£2 million ÷ £0.25 million = 8).

3) Managers compare this payback period with other projects and choose which project to go ahead with.

Advantages of Payback Period Calculation:	It's **easy** to **calculate** and **understand**. It's very good for **high risk** or **high tech** projects.
Disadvantages of Payback Period Calculation:	It ignores **cash flow** after payback. It ignores the **time value** of money.

> If you're wondering what the "time value" of money is, look on the next page.

Accounting Rate of Return (ARR) compares Yearly Profit with Investment

1) **Accounting rate of return** (ARR) compares the **average annual profit** with the level of investment — the higher the ARR, the more **favourable** the project will appear.

2) ARR is expressed as a **percentage** and calculated by:

$$\frac{\text{Average Annual Profit}}{\text{Investment}} \times 100\%$$

Example:

	Investment	Annual Profits				
		Year 1	Year 2	Year 3	Year 4	Year 5
Project A	(£10M)	£4M	£5M	£6M	£7M	£5M
Project B	(£8M)	£3M	£3M	£4M	£6M	£6M

> Project A pays back during year 3. It costs £10M, by the end of year 2 it's returned £9M and by the end of year 3 it's returned £15M. Project B also pays back its £8M investment some time in year 3.

The payback period for both these projects is the same, so you need to use **accounting rate of return**.

Project A (£10M investment) has a profit of (£M) 4 + 5 + 6 + 7 + 5 - 10 = **£17M**.

Average annual profit is £17M divided by the five years = **£3.4M**

ARR = £3.4M / £10M investment x 100% = <u>34%</u>

Project B (£8M investment) has a profit of (£M) 3 + 3 + 4 + 6 + 6 - 8 = **£14M**

Average annual profit is £14M ÷ 5 years = **£2.8M**

ARR = £2.8M / £8M investment x 100% = <u>35%</u>

> If they were only considering ARR (in real life they would also take into account other factors), the managers would choose project B because it has a higher ARR, just. Just. By a whisker.

Advantages of Average Rate of Return:	It's **easy** to **calculate** and **understand**. It takes account of all the project's cash flows.
Disadvantages of Average Rate of Return:	It ignores the timing of the **cash flows** (although it breaks them down by year). It ignores the **time value** of money.

Investment Decisions

The **Future Value** of cash inflow depends on **Risk** and **Opportunity Cost**

If someone offers you £100 cash in hand **now** or in one year's time, you'd do best to take it now. This is because of the **time value of money**. It's the principle of money being worth less if you wait for it, because of risk and opportunity cost.

1) There's a **risk** that the person would never pay you the £100 after a year had gone by.

2) In a year's time it'd be worth less due to **inflation**. You wouldn't be able to buy as much stuff with that £100.

3) There's an **opportunity cost** — you could **invest** the money instead of **waiting** for it. A high interest account would beat the rate of inflation and give you **even more value** than the £100 in your hand today. See p.31 and p.68 for more on this.

> A payment after a year or two, or three, is **always worth less** than the **same payment** made to you **today**.

Non-Numerical, **Qualitative** factors affect **Investment Decisions**

The investment decisions made by managers are based on a wide range of numerical data and quantitative methods. Managers must also put the decisions into a **qualitative** context, based on internal factors and market uncertainty.

Business Objectives and Strategy Can Influence Investment Decisions

1) An investment appraisal recommended purely on financial data **may not fit in** with the **objectives** of a firm. Many businesses will only make an investment if the project will **help them achieve** their objectives. E.g. a business which aims to produce **low cost products** for a large mass market (e.g. teaspoons) would be unlikely to invest **as much** in **research and development** as a high-end technology business.

Corporate Image Can Influence Investment Decisions

1) **Good corporate image** brings **customer goodwill** and **loyalty** in the long term. Investment decisions that create bad publicity and damage customer loyalty will damage the business in the **long term** — e.g. a firm with a green, **ecologically friendly** image would avoid investments that would damage the environment.

Industrial Relations Can Influence Investment Decisions

1) Investments which result in a **loss of jobs** may be turned down, even if they show a good rate of return.

2) **Loss of jobs** affects **staff morale**. The cost of **redundancy payments** should be factored into the decision. Trade unions may **strike** over the job losses, which would affect **productivity**. **Corporate image** may also be damaged.

The Market is Always Risky— and Each Project Has a Risk of Failure

1) The market is an environment that has **risk** and **uncertainty** every day. **Currency exchange rates** may alter, **sales** may decrease/increase, **customers' tastes** may change and **competitors** may become stronger.

2) Also, **each project** has specific **risk** — e.g. a new product might not sell very well. Every firm has a **different attitude** to **risk**.

Practice Questions

Q1 What does ARR take account of that payback doesn't?

Q2 Give one advantage and one disadvantage of ARR.

Q3 What is the risk of waiting two years to be paid £1000?

Q4 Give three examples of qualitative factors that might affect investment decisions.

Exam Question

Answer on p.108.

Q1 A business is investing in a new product. The initial investment is £200 000. The product will generate revenue of £100 000 per year, and costs of £60 000 per year. Calculate the accounting rate of return on the investment. (4 marks)

You have to speculate if you want to accumulate...

The key point to remember here is that if someone offers you £100, you should take it and run, before they change their mind. The other key point to remember is that businesses try to balance risk and return. They want to make as much money as possible, but if they take too many risks, they could end up losing the money they invested in the first place.

Company Accounts: Profit and Loss Account

The profit and loss account is a very useful collection of financial information. Interesting, too, if you like that sort of thing. **These pages are for OCR and WJEC, but may be useful if you're doing Edexcel too.**

Profit and Loss Accounts show Revenue and Expenses

1) The profit and loss account shows how much money's been **coming into the company** (**revenue**) and how much has been **going out** (**expenses**).

2) Revenue is **sales income** (turnover) from selling goods and services. This includes **cash payments** received and sales on **credit**.

   Sales income is recorded when the sale's made, not when the customer pays.

3) Expenses are all the **costs** of the business. These are divided into **direct** or **indirect** costs, and **fixed** or **variable** costs (see p.30).

4) Profit and loss accounts show revenue expenditure, and balance sheets show capital expenditure.

Here's what the Profit and Loss Account looks like

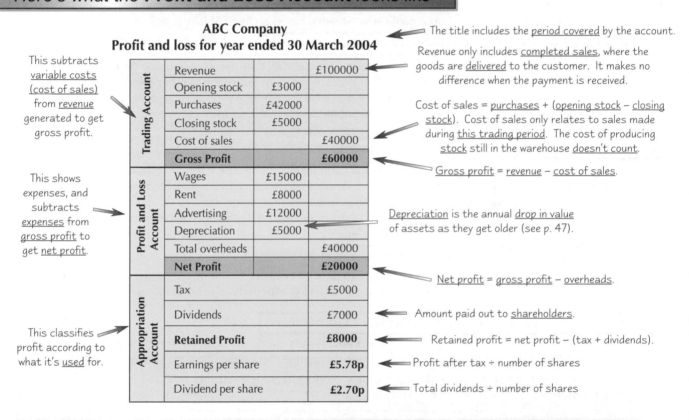

ABC Company
Profit and loss for year ended 30 March 2004

The title includes the period covered by the account.

This subtracts variable costs (cost of sales) from revenue generated to get gross profit.

Revenue only includes completed sales, where the goods are delivered to the customer. It makes no difference when the payment is received.

Trading Account	Revenue		£100000
	Opening stock	£3000	
	Purchases	£42000	
	Closing stock	£5000	
	Cost of sales		£40000
	Gross Profit		**£60000**
Profit and Loss Account	Wages	£15000	
	Rent	£8000	
	Advertising	£12000	
	Depreciation	£5000	
	Total overheads		£40000
	Net Profit		**£20000**
Appropriation Account	Tax		£5000
	Dividends		£7000
	Retained Profit		**£8000**
	Earnings per share		**£5.78p**
	Dividend per share		**£2.70p**

Cost of sales = purchases + (opening stock – closing stock). Cost of sales only relates to sales made during this trading period. The cost of producing stock still in the warehouse doesn't count.

Gross profit = revenue – cost of sales.

This shows expenses, and subtracts expenses from gross profit to get net profit.

Depreciation is the annual drop in value of assets as they get older (see p. 47).

Net profit = gross profit – overheads.

Amount paid out to shareholders.

This classifies profit according to what it's used for.

Retained profit = net profit – (tax + dividends).

Profit after tax ÷ number of shares

Total dividends ÷ number of shares

Profit = Revenue – Expenses (and there are different categories of profit...)

1) **Gross profit** is **revenue** minus **variable costs**. These variable costs are called the **cost of sales** on the profit and loss account.

2) **Net profit** is **gross profit** minus **fixed costs** (see p. 40 for more on gross and net profit).

3) **Operating profit** takes into account all revenues and costs from **regular trading**, but not any revenues and costs from **one-off** events. It only covers activities that are likely to be **repeated year on year**.

4) **Net profit before tax** covers **all revenues and costs**, including those from **one-off events** such as the sale or purchase of another business.

5) **Net profit after tax** is what's left after corporation tax has been paid.

6) **Retained profit** is what's left from net profit after tax, once **share dividends** have been paid to shareholders.

Gina was mainly interested in operating profit.

Company Accounts: Profit and Loss Account

The Profit and Loss Account is Three accounts in One

1) The **trading account** works out **gross profit** — revenue minus variable costs.

2) The **profit and loss account** subtracts overheads (fixed costs) to work out **operating profit** and **net profit**.

3) The **appropriation account** shows what's done with profits — it's either **distributed** between shareholders, or **kept** in the business to invest in future activities. The appropriation account works out **retained profit**.

Profit and Loss Accounts show Profits over a period of Time

1) Profit and loss accounts should cover one whole accounting year — otherwise they can be **misleading**. E.g. high street retailers can generate **half their annual revenue** in the lead-up to **Christmas** — a profit and loss account ignoring this period would give a very inaccurate picture of the business.

2) Profit and loss accounts usually contain the **previous year's data** (or the previous five years' data) as well, for **easy comparison** to see what's changed. It's very useful to be able to spot trends in turnover, costs and profits.

Stakeholders have an Interest in the Profit and Loss Account

1) **Managers** use the profit and loss account to judge **business performance**. They're interested in the **cost of sales** compared with **sales revenue** — the **higher** the **cost of sales**, the **lower** the **gross profit**.

2) **Employees** are interested in how much **profit** the business is making, as an indicator of **job security** and potential **pay rises**. They'll be especially interested in profits if there's a **profit-related** link in their pay scheme.

3) Shareholders want to know the company's **turnover**, and the **operating profit**, so that they can see how the company is **performing** compared to previous years.

4) Shareholders also like to check **profit appropriation**. Some shareholders like to get as much **dividend** as possible for a short-term return. Some prefer to see money being **reinvested** into the business for long-term returns.

5) Limited companies and partnerships with a turnover over £15 million have to submit their accounts to the **Inland Revenue**. The tax man is interested in **net profit** before tax, because that's what a business is **taxed** on. The Inland Revenue also check through the accounts to make sure that the accounts procedure is up to standard.

Profit and Loss Accounts can be Manipulated

1) The profit and loss account can be legally **manipulated** so that the business seems to be performing **better** than it actually is doing — this is called **window dressing**.

2) Businesses can put a **low** estimate on **depreciation**, especially on depreciation of **intangible** assets — assets that aren't physical objects, e.g. brands, patents and copyright.

3) A business could **sell off** some of its equipment or machinery (e.g. lorries) and **lease** (rent) it back — that way they get a lump sum payment that they can put onto the profit and loss account as an **income**.

Charlie hoped that if he could distract the shareholders with his outfit, they wouldn't notice that he'd manipulated the accounts.

4) Businesses sometimes classify **operating expenditure** (which is an **expense** on the **profit and loss account**) as **capital expenditure** (a **fixed asset** on the **balance sheet**). Balance sheet assets look **good**, and can be **depreciated** over several years, so the expenditure doesn't hit the profit and loss account all at once.

Practice Questions

Q1 What is operating profit?

Q2 What is retained profit?

Q3 What's the appropriation account?

Q4 Which parts of the profit and loss account are shareholders most interested in?

Exam Question

Q1 Discuss whether the profit and loss account gives a good indication of the financial wellbeing of a business. (12 marks)

Step 1: buy stuff. Step 2: sell stuff. Step 3: PROFIT...

Well, that's the simplest way of looking at business, I suppose. What the exam boards expect you to know about profit for this section is not so much how it's made, but what kind of profit it is. Profit can be gross, net, retained or operating. If you don't know what one or other of those terms mean, you need to revise these pages again. Ah, go on...

Company Accounts: Balance Sheet

Ah, the beautiful balance sheet. It's the closest that one piece of paper can get to telling you everything you need to know about a business. **These pages are for OCR and WJEC.**

Balance Sheets are lists of Assets and Liabilities

1) Balance sheets are a **snapshot** of a firm's finances at a **fixed point in time**. They show the value of all the **assets** (the things that belong to the business, including cash in the bank) and all the **liabilities** (the money the business owes). They also show the value of all the **capital** (see p.12) in the business, and the source of that capital — they show where the money's **come from** as well as what's being **done** with it.

2) The **value** of the **assets** purchased **equals** the **amount of money** used to **buy** them. Balance sheets... **balance.**

Balance Sheets show the Short-Term Financial Status of the Company

1) The balance sheet shows you how much the business is **worth**.

2) **Working capital** (net current assets) is the amount of money the business has available in the short term.

3) **Suppliers** are particularly interested in **working capital** and **liquidity**. They can look at the balance sheet to see how liquid the firm's assets are, as well as how much working capital the firm has. The more liquid the assets, the better the firm will be at paying bills. This helps them decide whether to offer the business supplies on **credit**, and how much credit to offer.

> Liquidity = how easy it is to pay debt. The liquidity of an asset is how easy it is to turn it into cash and spend it. Cash is the most liquid asset, then money owed by debtors, then stock, then short-term investments.

4) The balance sheet shows **sources of capital**. Ideally, **long-term loans** or **mortgages** are used to finance the purchase of fixed assets. A well-managed business wouldn't borrow too much through **short-term overdrafts**, because overdrafts are an expensive way of borrowing.

Assets are things the Business Owns (that it's bought with capital)

1) Assets includes **machinery**, **stock**, **property**, **land**, and **cash**, as well as money owed to the business by **debtors**.

2) Assets can be classified as **fixed assets** or **current assets**. Fixed assets are kept for more than a year — e.g. property, land and computers. They usually lose value each year (this is depreciation — see p.46-47). Current assets are likely to be exchanged for cash within the accounting year, before the next balance sheet is worked out — e.g. stock and money owed by debtors.

3) Assets can also be classified as **tangible** or **intangible**. **Tangible assets** are **actual physical stuff** such as property, stock or machinery. **Intangible assets** are **non-physical things** like brands, customer goodwill, patents and licences — the business has to **estimate** the value of these.

Interpreting balance sheets — Here's How It All Looks

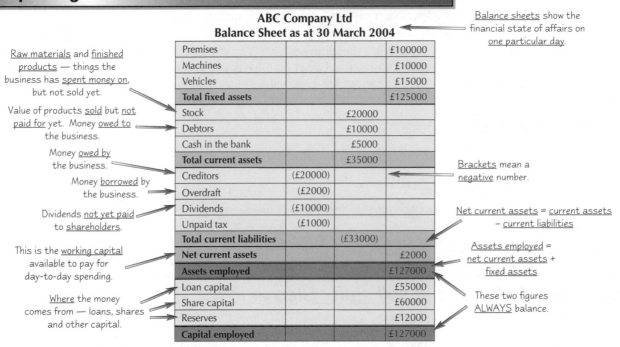

ABC Company Ltd
Balance Sheet as at 30 March 2004

Balance sheets show the financial state of affairs on one particular day.

Premises			£100000
Machines			£10000
Vehicles			£15000
Total fixed assets			**£125000**
Stock		£20000	
Debtors		£10000	
Cash in the bank		£5000	
Total current assets		**£35000**	
Creditors	(£20000)		
Overdraft	(£2000)		
Dividends	(£10000)		
Unpaid tax	(£1000)		
Total current liabilities		(£33000)	
Net current assets			**£2000**
Assets employed			**£127000**
Loan capital			£55000
Share capital			£60000
Reserves			£12000
Capital employed			**£127000**

Raw materials and finished products — things the business has spent money on, but not sold yet.

Value of products sold but not paid for yet. Money owed to the business.

Money owed by the business.

Money borrowed by the business.

Dividends not yet paid to shareholders.

This is the working capital available to pay for day-to-day spending.

Where the money comes from — loans, shares and other capital.

Brackets mean a negative number.

Net current assets = current assets – current liabilities

Assets employed = net current assets + fixed assets

These two figures ALWAYS balance.

Company Accounts: Balance Sheet

Bad Debts are debts that debtors Won't Ever Pay

1) Most debts owed to the business get paid, but some debtors **default** on their payments — they **don't pay up**.

2) Debts that don't get paid are called "**bad debts**". These bad debts **can't** be included on the balance sheet as an **asset** — because the business isn't going to get money for them.

3) The business **writes off** these bad debts, and puts them as an **expense** on the profit and loss account. This shows that the business has **lost money**.

Liabilities are Debts the Business Owes (where its capital has come from)

1) **Current liabilities** are **debts** which need to be paid off within a year, e.g. overdrafts and taxes.

2) **Long-term liabilities** are debts that the business will pay off over several years, e.g. mortgages and loans.

3) All the company's **sources of capital** count as a liability, even money invested by **shareholders**. This is because if the business ceased trading, the shareholders would want their money back. The owner's equity (money they've put in) counts as a liability for a **partnership** as well.

> **Liabilities = where the money's from.**
> **Assets = what you've done with it.**

4) **Reserves** are mostly retained profits, and also include money from any rises in asset value. Reserves count as a **liability** because they're a **source of finance**.

Accounts reflect Assets that Depreciate — they Lose Value over Time

1) The **drop in value** of a business asset over time is called **depreciation**.

2) Businesses **calculate depreciation** each year to make sure that an asset's **value** on the **balance sheet** is a **true reflection** of what the business would get from **selling** it. Spreading depreciation over several years' accounts **stops** it hitting **all at once** when the business **sells** the asset.

3) The **amount lost** through depreciation is recorded on the **profit and loss account** as an **expense**.

Balance Sheets can be Manipulated

1) Balance sheets can be **manipulated** with **window dressing** in the same way as profit and loss accounts (see p.45). Businesses can use **tricks** to make the business seem **better off** than it is.

2) Putting a **low** value on **depreciation** increases the value of **fixed assets** on the balance sheet.

3) Selling **fixed assets** and **leasing** them back makes the business seem more **solvent** (better able to survive) because it increases the amount of **cash** that the business actually has in the bank.

Practice Questions

Q1 Give two examples of fixed assets, and two examples of current assets.
Q2 What are bad debts?
Q3 Why is share capital classified as a liability?
Q4 Why do businesses depreciate their assets each year?

Exam Question

Q1 "It's impossible for asset valuations on the balance sheet to be 100% accurate". To what extent do you agree with this statement? (10 marks)

Liabilities = where the money's from. Assets = what the money's paid for...

Balance sheets can seem weird — why are reserves liabilities when cash is an asset, for example. If you see where the money's from, and what the firm's done with it, you can see what goes where and why it balances. Valuing the assets properly is the hard part — you have to learn how to do depreciation calculations, and how to deal with bad debts.

Business Structures

The structure of a business depends on its size, the product or service it offers and the culture of the organisation. It's nothing to do with the type of bricks they used to build head office. **For AQA, OCR, Edexcel and WJEC.**

Structure and Hierarchy are shown by an Organisational Chart

1) The traditional business structure is a series of levels, where each level has responsibility and authority over the levels below. This is called a **hierarchy**.

2) An **organisational chart** sets out who has **authority** to make decisions, and who has the **responsibility** for making them.

3) It shows whom individual employees are **accountable** to — who is directly **above** them in the hierarchy.

4) It shows who employees are **responsible** for — who is directly **below** them in the hierarchy.

5) The board of **directors** are **accountable** for making sure the **owner** of the business and other **stakeholders** make a **return** on their **investment**.

6) The chart also shows how the organisation is divided up. It can be divided by **function**, e.g. into a production department, a marketing department etc., or it can be divided by **product** or **geographical area**.

> **Board of Directors** — gives direction to the business.
> (Managing Director, Finance Director, Marketing Director, Production Director)
>
> **Managers** — make sure targets are met.
> (e.g. sales managers, finance managers, human resources managers, production managers)
>
> **Team Leaders** — Responsible for a team of supervisors and shop-floor workers.
>
> **Supervisors** — oversee things on a day-to-day basis.
>
> **Shop-floor Workers** — do the actual work.
> (e.g. sales reps, market researchers, production workers, etc.)

Matrix Structures organise staff by Task

1) Businesses with **matrix** structures divide employees into **teams**, with each team working on a **different project**.

2) Each team has **workers** with **different** areas of **expertise**, e.g. an engineer, a designer and a marketing expert.

3) One advantage of the matrix structure is that it ensures that staff are pursuing **clearly defined objectives**, and it **encourages** departments to build **relationships** with one another. However, because each member of a team has a project manager and a department manager, this structure can sometimes lead to **conflict**.

4) Firms which need **decisions** to be made **quickly** might have an **entrepreneurial** structure. A small **group** of **key staff** at the centre of the organisation make **all** the **decisions**. This method works **best** in **small companies**, where the key staff are aware of what is happening in all departments.

5) Some **joint ventures** have an **independent** management **structure**. This means that they are run by their **own management** team, **not** by the **management** of either of their **parent companies**. It tends to only be found in joint ventures which have been around for a while, and are **well-established**.

Structures can be "Tall" or "Flat"

1) Organisations with **lots of levels** in their hierarchy are called "**tall**". They have a large number of people between the top and the bottom. Tall structures have a long **chain of command**. The chain of command is the path of **communication** and **authority** up and down the hierarchy.

2) If the structure is **too tall**, it affects **communication**. Messages take a **long time** to get from one end of the chain of command to the other, and they can get **garbled** on the way. **Decisions** take a long time to make, and there's a lot of **paperwork** to deal with.

3) "**Flat**" organisations only have a few levels in the hierarchy. People may be given more responsibility and freedom.

4) If the structure is **too flat**, then managers can get **overwhelmed** by too many people reporting to them.

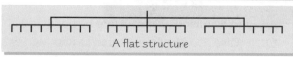

A tall structure

A flat structure

Structures can have broad or narrow Spans of Control

1) Managers in **flat** structures have **wide** spans of control. This means they have a **lot** of workers answering to them.

2) Managers in tall structures have **narrower** spans of control — they aren't responsible for as many people. This allows them to **monitor** the people who report to them **more closely**.

3) If the span of control is **too broad**, managers can find it hard to manage **effectively**.

4) If the span of control is **too narrow**, workers can become **demotivated** — they may feel that they're being **micromanaged** (over-managed) by interfering bosses.

5) **Traditionally**, business experts thought it would be hard for a manager to keep a close eye on workers when the span of control is bigger than about 6 people. But if the workers are all doing the **same routine task**, they don't need as much close supervision — so a span of control of 10-12 people (or more) is fine.

Business Structures

Centralised Structures keep Authority for decisions at the Top

In an organisation where decision-making is **centralised**, all decisions are made by **one person**, or one committee of **senior managers** right at the **top** of the business.

Advantages of Centralisation	Disadvantages of Centralisation
Business leaders tend to have plenty of **experience**.	Not many people are **expert** enough in **all aspects** of the business.
Managers get an **overview** of the whole business.	Excluding employees from decision-making can be **demotivating**.
Senior managers understand **central** budgeting restrictions and can make decisions to save the **whole business** money.	Decisions can take a **long time**. The organisation reacts **slowly** to change, and can end up a couple of steps behind its competitors.

Decentralised Structures share out the Authority to make decisions

1) Decentralisation **shares out authority** to more **junior** employees.

2) Giving responsibility for decision-making to people below you is called **delegation**. There's more about delegation on p.56.

3) **National** and **multinational** firms **decentralise** decision-making and delegate power to **regional** managers.

4) Managers have to make sure that the **work** of **all** a company's **employees** is **contributing** in some way to the **goals** of the **business**. This is called **management coordination**, and it can be **difficult** to achieve when a lot of **power** has been **delegated**.

Advantages of Decentralisation	Disadvantages of Decentralisation
Involvement in decision-making **motivates** employees.	Subordinates may not have enough **experience** to make decisions.
Employees can use **expert knowledge** of their sector.	**Inconsistencies** may develop between sectors in a business.
Decisions can be made more **quickly** without having to ask senior managers.	Junior employees may not be able to see the **overall situation** and **needs** of an organisation.

Delayering removes layers of hierarchy

Delayering is one of the key ways in which a manager might choose to **alter** the **structure** of a business. Changing the structure of the business can improve **performance** and increase **competitiveness**.

1) Delayering means removing a layer of the hierarchy — usually a layer of managers from around the middle.

2) Delayering helps to **lower costs**. Cutting management jobs can save a lot of money in salaries.

3) After delayering, you get a **flatter** structure with **broader** spans of control. If you **overdo** it, managers can end up **stressed** and overworked with **huge** spans of control.

4) Delayering can give junior employees **enhanced roles** with more responsibility.

5) Some businesses use delayering as an **excuse** to cut jobs.

Practice Questions

Q1 Why might a flat structure be popular with junior employees in a business?

Q2 What is meant by "span of control"?

Q3 Give two advantages of a centralised decision-making structure.

Q4 What is "delayering"? Give one reason why a business might delayer.

Exam Questions

Q1 A firm of management consultants have advised Douglas McLeod to delayer and flatten the structure of his business. Discuss the factors that Douglas should think about before starting to delayer. (12 marks)

Q2 To what extent is a wide span of control desirable for a manager in a business? (10 marks)

Delayering — isn't that taking off your cardigan when it's warm...

Delayering can be a great way of simplifying things and saving money — if your middle managers are a bunch of useless David Brent types, getting rid of them is the kindest thing to do, really. Both tall and flat structures have pros and cons — learn them in case you get asked to evaluate a particular kind of business structure.

Measuring Workforce Effectiveness

A business needs to measure the effectiveness of all its resources, including its workforce. And measuring your workforce isn't as simple as you might think. You can't even use a tape measure. **For all boards.**

Human Resource Management (HRM) *keeps the* Workforce Flexible

Businesses need to be **flexible** enough to react in a competitive and changing environment. Change comes from consumer **demand**, new **technology** and new **laws**. **Competitors** are constantly joining and leaving the market. A flexible workforce tends to be an effective one, so HRM makes sure that the workforce is **adaptable** to these changes.

1) The main function of Human resources is to ensure that the business has the **right number** of **employees** and that they're of the **right quality** in terms of **qualifications** and **skills**.

This is all called workforce planning.

2) HRM plans how to **recruit** staff — where to advertise, how to interview, etc.

3) **Human resources strategies** can be **short-term** (e.g. recruiting part-time staff for Christmas sales in retailing) or **long-term** (e.g. anticipating growth or a change in production techniques).

4) Human resources departments also decide how to treat staff while they're working for the business — how to **use their skills**, how to **keep** them working for the company, how to **train** and **reward** them, and eventually how to **terminate** their employment.

5) HRM makes sure that managers carry out regular staff **appraisals**. Appraisals are where **employees meet** with their **manager** to **discuss** how well they are **meeting goals** and to identify future **training needs**.

6) The HRM department might also set up a **performance management system** to check that human resources are always being used to maximum efficiency. This system calculates performance based on **labour productivity**, **absenteeism**, and **labour turnover**. If workers are not as productive as they could be, the business might **struggle** to **meet** its **objectives**.

For more on business objectives, see p.2.

Labour Productivity *measures* How Much *each* Employee Produces

It's important for companies to know how productive their workforce is, because changes in labour productivity can have a massive impact on the business. This is especially true in **labour intensive** firms, where labour costs are a high proportion of total costs.

$$\text{Labour Productivity} = \frac{\text{Output per period}}{\text{Number of employees}}$$

The **higher** the labour productivity, the **better** the workforce is performing. As labour productivity **increases**, labour costs per unit **fall**.

Dave's productivity currently stood at 900 rabbits per hour.

Example: A factory has 30 workers per shift working 3 shifts per day to produce 9000 DVD players per week.
Productivity = 9000 ÷ 90 workers = **100** DVD players per worker per week.

Ways to improve labour productivity

1) Labour productivity can be increased by **improving worker motivation** (see p.54-57).

2) **Training** can make workers more productive.

3) Labour productivity can also be improved by changing to **more efficient** methods of production — e.g. changing from job to batch production or from batch to flow production (see p.64-65). These gains need to be balanced against the **costs** of changing production method, and any **reduced production flexibility**.

4) Some companies **reward** increased productivity. Paying workers using a **piece rate** (see p.56) system encourages staff to produce more. Managers should take care that **quality** doesn't suffer in the process.

5) Increasing labour productivity means **redundancies** and **job losses** unless sales increase. Businesses need to **plan** for the consequences of improved productivity to avoid upsetting staff.

6) Businesses should **monitor** their labour productivity over time. When they're setting targets, they should compare their productivity to **competitors' productivity** through **benchmarking** (see p.67).

7) Businesses must **balance** productivity against things like product **quality** and long-term worker **motivation**.

Measuring Workforce Effectiveness

Absenteeism measures the Proportion of Time employees are Off Work

$$\text{Absenteeism} = \frac{\text{Number of staff days lost}}{\text{Number of working days}} \times 100\%$$

To calculate the number of working days, multiply the number of days that a company operates by its total number of employees.

1) Absenteeism is measured as a percentage. Obviously, **low** is best.

2) You have to analyse figures in the **context** of each industry. For example, **police** officers might have **higher** than average figures because of the dangers and stresses of the job, while **sales** people paid on commission have **lower** rates because they lose pay when they're off work.

3) **Causes** of absenteeism include poor **working conditions**, poor **relationships** with managers and other staff, **stress** or **disillusionment** with the job, and poor **motivation**.

4) Absenteeism **increases costs**. It results in **lost opportunities**, e.g. sales enquiries left unanswered.

5) There are several ways a firm might **reduce absenteeism**, depending on what's causing it. These might include **job enrichment** (see p.56), improving **working relationships**, improving **working conditions**, or **flexi-time**.

Labour Turnover measures the Proportion of Staff who Leave each year

$$\text{Labour Turnover} = \frac{\text{Number of staff leaving}}{\text{Average number of staff employed}} \times 100\%$$

Work out the part-timers as if they were fractions of a full-time employee. Two people who each work half a week = one person working a whole week.

1) The **higher** the figure, the larger the proportion of workers leaving the firm each year.

2) **External causes** of high labour turnover include changes in regional **unemployment** levels, and the growth of other local firms using staff with **similar skills**.

3) **Internal causes** of high labour turnover include poor motivation of staff, low wages, and a lack of opportunities for promotion. Staff will **join other firms** to increase their pay and job responsibilities.

4) A **poor recruitment** process which selects weak candidates will also increase labour turnover.

5) Increased **delegation**, **job enrichment**, higher **wages** and better **training** can reduce employee turnover.

6) Labour turnover of 0 means no one **ever** leaves. Businesses need **some** labour turnover to bring new ideas in, and to keep the workforce flexible. **Natural wastage** (see p.53) can be useful if a firm needs to **reduce** labour **costs**, although it may also be necessary to make some staff **redundant**. Staff are usually only **dismissed** if they have done something **wrong**.

Dismissal and redundancy are not the same thing.

Benefits of high staff turnover	Disadvantages of high staff turnover
Constant stream of **new ideas** through new staff.	Lack of **loyal** and **experienced** staff who know the business.
Firm can recruit staff who've **already been trained** by competitors — saves money.	Firm **loses** staff it has **trained**, often to direct competitors.
If sales fall, firm can reduce workforce through **natural wastage** rather than costly redundancy.	**Training costs money** and **productivity drops** while new staff get trained.
Enthusiasm of new staff influences other workers.	**Recruitment** costs are high.

Practice Questions

Q1 A company has low labour productivity. Make three suggestions that might help to increase its output.

Q2 A firm operates for 245 days per year. It has 56 staff. In 2006, staff were absent for a total of 274 staff days. Calculate the firm's absenteeism.

Answer on p.108.

Q3 State two benefits and two drawbacks of a high labour turnover percentage.

Exam Questions

Q1 Explain why a major employer such as the NHS should be concerned about differing absenteeism percentages in different hospitals, and recommend what action they could take. (10 marks)

Q2 Evaluate potential problems if a firm were to change its production method to improve labour productivity. (6 marks)

I have a flexible workforce — they're always bending the rules...

They're all quite easy really, these equations. Problem is, the numbers alone don't really tell you anything. It's good to have high productivity if you're making something simple, like baked beans, but not necessarily if the product is complicated — a jet plane, for example. The same can't be said for absenteeism though — that's always a bad thing...

Workforce Planning

Businesses try to create a flexible workforce by investing in recruitment and training. **For all boards.**

Businesses need to **Plan** their **Employment Needs**

1) Businesses need to work out how many employees they need, both now and in the **future**.
   They also have to make sure that their employees have the right skills for the needs of the business.

2) Finding people with the right **skills** to do a particular job can be expensive and time-consuming,
   but it usually pays off in the long run. Most companies have a recruitment process to help them
   employ the staff they need. There are usually **seven** steps to the recruitment process:

Identify vacancy → Write person specification and job description → Advertise job → Applications received → Shortlist most suitable candidates → Interview most suitable candidates → Appointment of most suitable candidate

3) There are several different ways that a business can identify a vacancy:

   a) HRM departments ask **other experienced managers** for their **opinions** and **advice**.

   b) **Past statistics** (backdata) are used to see if employee numbers have **risen**, **fallen** or **stayed the same**.

   c) An increase or decrease in **demand** for a **product** means an increase or decrease in the **need for workers**.

   d) HRM analyses the **current staff details** to see how many people might **leave** or **retire** in the near future.

   e) The introduction of **new techniques** (e.g. automation) will alter the number of workers needed.

   f) Businesses do an **internal audit**. They look at all the **jobs** in the organisation, what each job entails
      and what sort of **skills** are needed. They then see whether current staff **match** these requirements.

Businesses can recruit **Internally** or **Externally**

Internal recruitment is recruiting people who **already** work for the business.
External recruitment is recruiting people from **outside** the company.

Advantages of internal recruitment	1) Managers **know** the internal candidates. 2) Internal candidates **know the business** and its objectives. 3) It's a **shorter** and **less expensive** process than external recruitment. 4) It **motivates** workers by encouraging them to go for promotion.
Disadvantages of internal recruitment	1) Internal promotion leaves **another vacancy** to be filled. 2) It can cause **resentment** among colleagues who aren't selected.
Advantages of external recruitment	1) External recruits bring in **fresh new ideas**. 2) External recruits bring **experience** from other organisations. 3) There's a larger pool of applicants to **choose** from.
Disadvantages of external recruitment	1) Managers **don't know** the applicant. 2) It's usually a **long** and **expensive** process. 3) External recruits usually need a longer **induction** process (see p.53).

Some firms prefer to recruit people with a positive attitude towards the job even if they'll need a bit more training than other candidates.

Selection — getting the **Right People** for the job

To have the best chance of getting the best person for the job, the HR department **analyses** the
vacancy and draws up a **job description** and a **person specification**.

1) The **job description** lists the tasks and responsibilities the person appointed will be expected to carry out. It
   may also state the job title, the location, the nature of the business and other details like salary and conditions
   (e.g. holiday entitlement, pension arrangements and so on).

2) The **person specification** outlines the ideal profile of the person needed to match the job description. It
   describes their **qualifications**, experience, interests and **personality**. It's important to know if the candidate
   will fit into the **culture** and **atmosphere** of the business, as well as knowing what qualifications they've got.

Methods of selection include **Interviews** and **Tests**

1) **Interviews** are the most common way of choosing candidates. Candidates can be interviewed **one-to-one**
   or by a **panel** of interviewers. Phone interviews are thought to be less effective than **face-to-face** interviews.

2) Some organisations use **assessment centres** to help them **test** candidates. Tests include **psychometric** testing
   which assesses personality fit, **aptitude** tests which find out how good the candidate is at job tasks, and
   group exercises which show how candidates interact with other people in various situations.

Workforce Planning

Employees need Training and Development

1) The **first day** or so on the job is usually spent introducing people to the organisation — learning the workings of the business, covering health and safety issues, and meeting key staff. This is the **induction** part of the HR cycle.

2) Most new employees need some training — either to learn **new skills** or **improve** and **update** existing skills.

3) Training can be done **off-the-job** — e.g. studying part-time at a local **college**, a short one or two day **course** at a business training centre, or **studying at home** for a professional qualification.

4) Training can be done **on-the-job** — i.e. in the workplace.

This is rather endearingly called "sitting next to Nellie".

On-the-job training can take several forms:

1) The **traditional** way is to sit the new trainee next to an **experienced worker**. The newbie watches and learns from the experienced worker, who is there to answer any questions about the job.

2) **Mentoring** is where the new employee is advised by an experienced worker who acts as **tutor** and guru.

3) **Coaching** gives the trainee **specialised** knowledge and skills, e.g. through **seminars** or **group sessions**.

4) **Job rotation** is where the new person **moves around** the organisation and experiences **different jobs**.

Off-the-job Training can be Expensive

Advantages of **on-the-job** training	1) On-the-job training is **easy** to **organise**. 2) **Costs** of training tend to be **lower**. 3) Training is **specific** to the job in question.
Disadvantages of **on-the-job** training	1) **Trainer** and **trainee** are **not productive** during training hours. 2) The **trainer** may **not** be skilled in **communication** or have other **weaknesses**. 3) **Bad** work **practices** can be **passed on** to the trainee. 4) **New ways** of **working** are **not introduced** into the company.

The type of training is determined by the **size** and **type** of business and by the **job** that the trainee is employed to do.

Businesses should **evaluate** their training to see how it's **working**, using clear, measurable objectives. Managers should be able to **compare training costs** with the **financial gains** in overall performance using **cost-benefit analysis**.

Advantages of **off-the-job** training	1) Off-the-job training uses **specialist trainers**. 2) Training can be more **intensive**. 3) **New theories** and **practices** can be **introduced** to the business. 4) Training occurs **away** from the **distractions** of the job.
Disadvantages of **off-the-job** training	1) Off-the-job training is more **expensive**. 2) The trainee might **not** have **access** to **specific tools** used in their job. 3) The trainee is **off-site** and is **not productive**.

Severance is what happens when an Employee Leaves

— *OCR and Edexcel* —

1) **Severance** is the point at which an **employee ends** their **contract** with the company. It can be caused by **natural wastage** (people who choose to leave), or by **redundancy** or **dismissal**.

2) **Staff** are **made redundant** if the firm **no longer requires** people to do a **particular job function**. Redundancies can be **compulsory**, or, if a company needs to make lots of people redundant, it might offer **financial incentives** for **voluntary redundancies** — people who volunteer to leave. People who've been made redundant are entitled to a **redundancy payment** — the **amount varies** depending on **how long** they've worked for the firm.

3) People should only be **dismissed** (sacked) if they've **failed** to **do** their **job** properly or **broken** company **rules**.

— *OCR and Edexcel* — *OCR and Edexcel* —

OCR and Edexcel

Practice Questions

Q1 Briefly explain the terms "job description" and "person specification".

Q2 Explain the difference between on-the-job training and off-the-job training.

Q3 List and describe three methods of on-the-job training.

Exam Questions

Q1 Describe the process a company needs to go through when recruiting new staff. (4 marks)

Q2 Evaluate the advantages and disadvantages of internal and external recruitment for a retail organisation with 200 stores nationwide. (15 marks)

Internal Recruitment — sounds painful...

Recruitment and training can use up a lot of time and money. They're worth doing properly though, because the additional costs tend to pay off in the long run. A well-chosen employee will work harder and stick around for longer (as long as they're being well trained) so hopefully it'll be a while before you have to go through the whole process again.

Motivating the Workforce

Motivation is important in business — motivated employees get more done than non-motivated employees. The theorists on these pages tried to work out what motivates people. **For all boards.**

1) Taylor and Scientific Management — people are in it for the Money

1) In the early 20th century, FW Taylor thought that workers were motivated by **money**. He believed workers would do the **minimum** amount of work if left to their own devices.

2) Taylor developed his theories through **work-study** — watching how people work. He did **time and motion studies**, timing work activities with a **stopwatch**. This allowed him to figure out the **most efficient** way to do a job, and then make sure every single worker did it that way. He favoured **division of labour** — breaking work down into a lot of **small repetitive tasks**. This approach is called **scientific management**.

3) Taylor believed in paying workers according to the **quantity** they produced — the most **productive** workers got a **better rate**. He believed that financial incentives would **motivate** workers and raise **productivity**.

4) Scientific management didn't go down well with workers. Increased productivity meant that **fewer workers** were needed — workers worried about losing their jobs.

5) There were other disadvantages, too — increased productivity could lead to a reduction in **quality**. **Supervisors** were needed to monitor efficiency and for quality control purposes.

6) Taylor's approach wouldn't work for modern businesses — it would be seen as **exploitation**. It also ignores the **demotivating** effect of doing very repetitive boring work.

2) Mayo and Human Relations — people are motivated by Social Factors

OCR, AQA and WJEC

1) Elton Mayo found that people achieved more when they got **positive attention**. Mayo was doing an experiment on productivity when he found that **all** workers taking part in the experiment became more productive. He worked out that this was because they liked the **social contact** that they got from the experiments, and they liked working in a **group**.

2) Mayo thought management should **pay attention** to workers as individuals, and **involve** them in decision-making. He thought that firms should try to make business goals compatible with workers' goals. This required a **democratic** style of management, as well as lots of **delegation** and good **communication**.

3) He also thought that workers should **socialise** together — outside work as well as at work.

OCR, AQA and WJEC — *OCR, AQA and WJEC*

3) Maslow's Hierarchy of Needs — people need Basics first

Maslow said that people start by meeting the needs at the **bottom** of the pyramid. Once they've sorted out those needs, they can move on to the needs on the **next level** up.

Maslow and Herzberg both believed that workers had needs which were specific to them as individuals.

- **Self-actualisation** meeting potential — Businesses meet these needs by giving the opportunity to develop new skills and take responsibility.
- **Self-esteem** — achievement — Businesses give employees recognition and offer promotion.
- **Social Needs** — friendship, teamwork — Teamworking and social outings are designed to meet these.
- **Safety** — safe work environment with job security — Health and safety policy and secure employment contracts meet these needs.
- **Basic Physical Needs** — food, water, shelter, clothes — Businesses meet these needs by paying workers enough and providing a warm, dry work environment.

The pyramid **looks good** — but it isn't always **obvious** which level an individual is at.

4) Herzberg's Hygiene and Motivating factors — sort out a Good Environment first

In the 1960s, Frederick Herzberg interviewed accountants and engineers to find out what motivated and satisfied them at work. He identified two groups of factors which influenced the motivation of workers:

1) **Hygiene factors** are things like good **company policy**, **supervision**, **working conditions**, **pay**, and **relations** with fellow employees. They don't motivate as such, but if they **aren't good**, workers get **dissatisfied**.

2) **Motivating factors** are things like **interesting work**, personal **achievement**, **recognition** of achievement, and scope for more **responsibility** and personal **development**. These factors **do** positively motivate workers.

Motivating the Workforce

5) Drucker and Management by Objectives — companies need Clear Goals — OCR

1) In his book **The Practice of Management**, Peter Drucker said that both **companies** and **managers** need to have a clear **long-term strategy**. This strategy can then be broken down into **smaller goals** for the rest of the **workforce**. This method is called **Management by Objectives (MBO)**.

2) Businesses which use the Management by Objectives method usually have **two sets** of **managers**. A group of elite **senior managers** sets the **objectives** for specialised **departmental managers**.

3) Drucker also said that if a business had a **clear structure**, this would lead to **better performance**.

4) Many people think Drucker's theories are **accurate** because he developed them after observing **large corporations** such as General Motors and IBM. This means they are much more **business-specific** than the ideas of other theorists such as Maslow.

5) MBO is **less popular** than it was a **few years ago**, because of the way it only allows **ideas** to come from the **top** of the **organisational structure**. Companies which still manage in this way now tend to allow **workers** at the **bottom** of the hierarchy to put forward suggestions for both **long-** and **short-term strategy**.

Denise wasn't really a manager — she was just practising.

6) Peters' Excellence Model — people need to be aware of a Company's Values

1) Tom **Peters** claimed that if workers were treated well, and given **autonomy** (the freedom to decide how they work), they would give **excellent performance**.

2) Peters argued that the word '**management**' should be **abandoned**, and **replaced** by 'leadership'. The **leaders** of a company are **responsible** for **encouraging staff**.

3) He said that managers should **value workers**, but should have **high expectations** of what they are able to achieve.

4) To make sure that workers are contributing to the aims of the business, management must make employees **aware** of the company's **values** and **culture**.

5) Once employees know the company's values, **decision-making** can be **delegated** to them.

6) Ideally, companies should stay **small** and concentrate on what they **know best** — this prevents people from feeling left out and **alienated**.

— OCR — OCR —

Practice Questions

Q1 Give a brief description of Taylor's views on motivation.
Q2 Put the following needs in ascending order according to Maslow's hierarchy: friendship, job security, achievement.
Q3 Who invented MBO? Why is it no longer as popular as it used to be?
Q4 What did Peters think managers needed to do to achieve excellent performance from staff?

Exam Questions

Q1 A coffee-shop owner has a workforce made up of women with children, and part-time students. Suggest how he could best increase motivation levels among his staff, giving reasons for your choices. (10 marks)

Q2 John Rogers has been using the MBO method to manage his company. However, in recent months, lots of staff have left and production levels have fallen among the remaining staff. Explain why this might be and suggest ways in which he could improve morale within his workforce. (10 marks)

Sandwiches with Mayo increase productivity — no, really, they do...

It's the social factor, you see — people like eating them together. Right, back to the point. . . the theories of motivation. You won't be tested on who said what, but the ideas might well come in handy for giving examples of how managers today could increase the motivation of their workforce. Believe it or not, people aren't just in it for the money...

Motivating the Workforce

The work of the motivational theorists means that in the modern workplace there are loads of incentives designed to make people work harder. Some are financial, others aren't. **This page is for all boards.**

Modern Managers can learn from the Motivational Theorists

Many of the ideas put forward by motivational theorists can be useful for managers in businesses today.

1) Lots of businesses try hard to satisfy their employees' **social needs**. Many companies now have **sporting facilities** or organise **trips** outside of work. However, out of all Mayo's ideas, **teamwork** is the one that is still **most used** today.

2) If staff seem to be suffering from poor motivation, modern managers might **change** their **leadership style** (for more on leadership, see p.58).

3) Although **Taylor's ideas** are mostly considered **outdated**, **aspects** of them have **survived**. **Piece rate pay** is based on his ideas, and the role of the **supervisor** is now quite common.

Nerys increased motivation by volunteering to wear the turquoise Spandex pants.

Financial Incentives are used to Reward and Motivate

Most working people in the UK get paid a monthly **salary** or a weekly **wage**. There are other kinds of financial motivation, like **commission** and **fringe benefits**.

1) Workers who are paid a **weekly wage** get a set rate of so many **pounds per hour**. The more hours they work the more they get paid. There's a minimum wage — in 2007 it was £5.52 per hour for those aged 22 and over. Workers usually work a **fixed working week** of about 40 hours, and get paid more for any **overtime** they work.

2) Workers who get paid a monthly **salary** get so many **thousand pounds a year**, divided into 12 monthly payments. The salary isn't directly related to the number of hours worked — salaried employees work a minimum number of hours a week, and then as many hours as it takes to get the job done.

3) **Piecework** is where **production workers** are paid by **piece rate** — they get paid so many pounds or pence **per finished item** (or set quantity). The more the worker produces, the more they get paid.

4) Salespeople are usually paid **commission** — a **percentage** of the **sales** they achieve. Most sales staff get a low **basic salary** and earn commission on top of that, but some get commission only.

5) **Performance-related pay** gives more money to employees who meet their targets. Performance-related pay is linked in with employee **appraisals**. Some employees worry that they won't get a performance-related pay rise if they don't get on particularly well with the manager doing the appraisal interviews.

6) In addition to weekly/monthly pay, employees may get **fringe benefits**. These can include a **staff discount** for company products (common in retail, not so common in aircraft manufacturing...), employer contributions to employee **pensions**, private **medical insurance**, a company **car**, **profit-sharing** schemes and **shares** in the company.

7) Some companies give their employees a **bonus** if they **meet** or **exceed** their **targets**.

8) Companies have to be able to afford to offer financial incentives. **New companies** are often **not able** to offer **financial incentives** until they're sure how much profit they will make.

Non-Financial Motivation — Jobs are Designed to be more Satisfying

Lots of businesses today design jobs to be motivating. A well-designed job has **varied job tasks** and gives employees some **control** over their work. It will also try to include as many of **Herzberg's motivating factors** as possible, e.g.:

1) **Job enlargement** gives the employee more work at the same level. It's also called **horizontal loading**.

2) **Job enrichment** gives workers more **challenging** work, and the **training** they need to do it. It gives employees more responsibility for organising their work and solving problems. It's also called **vertical loading**.

3) **Teamworking** puts workers into small teams and lets them organise their own work. In recent years, many firms have begun organising employees into teams, which is why organisational structures often include **team leaders.**

4) **Empowerment** gives employees more **control** over their working day, and a greater role in **decision-making** — e.g. **quality circles** allow small groups of workers from various departments to meet and suggest **improvements** to productivity and quality.

5) **Consultation** and **delegation** both involve the employee in **decision-making**. **Consultation** is when **employees** are **asked** for their **views** on **decisions** which affect them, although the actual decisions are made by a manager. **Delegation** means that managers give their **employees** the **authority** to **make** certain **decisions** by themselves.

6) **Flexible working** helps to motivate people who find it difficult to balance their work and home lives because of other commitments — it allows them to work **part-time**, on a **temporary** basis, or **irregular hours** (e.g. not 9-5).

Motivating the Workforce

The *Organisational Structure* affects which *Motivational Techniques* are used

1) Companies which have a **tall** structure are more likely to use **pay** to motivate people. **Communication** in tall structures can be **poor**, so it's **difficult** for them to use methods like **empowerment** and **consultation**.

2) Organisations with a **flat** structure tend to be better at focusing on the **needs** of the **individual**, so they might motivate people through job **enlargement** or **enrichment**. **Communication** is **easier**, so staff are often involved in **decision-making** — **delegation** and **empowerment** are common.

3) An organisation with a **flat** structure might **not** want to introduce **team working**, because having **team leaders** introduces an **extra** level of **hierachy** and makes the structure taller.

It can be *Useful* to make *Changes* to the *Workforce*

WJEC

1) No workforce can stay the same for ever. **Growth** or **diversification** (changing what you do or the way that you do it) might **force** a company to **change** the way it operates.

2) A firm might also **choose** to **change** if it has been **operating** in the **same way** for a **long time**. If workers become **complacent**, they may not work hard to meet goals, which can cause a **drop** in **productivity**.

3) It's important to **manage** the **effects** of **change** on the workforce, to make sure it doesn't have a **negative effect** on their **motivation** or **effectiveness**.

4) Change can cause **workers** to become **resentful** or **insecure** — they might worry about learning **new methods** of working, or about **losing** their **jobs**.

5) A **change** of **staff** can also be **beneficial** — recruiting **employees** from **outside** the **company** can help to bring in **new ideas** (see p.52 for more on external recruitment).

Strong *Leadership* helps organisations to *Change*

1) People who work for effective leaders are usually more willing to **accept change**, because they tend to **trust** their managers and are well **motivated**.

2) Employees who trust the decisions of their manager may even want to take on some **responsibility** for making change happen.

3) A good leader might make change **less scary** for employees by breaking it down into **smaller**, more achievable **goals**.

4) Strong leaders **minimise** the **negative effects** of change. For example, if a company grows rapidly, it can become very **bureaucratic**, with too much paperwork as different departments try to keep in touch with one another. A good leader would introduce new methods of communication to prevent this from happening.

5) A strong leader is more likely to **recognise** the **need** for **change** in an organisation before external factors force change upon it.

WJEC   *WJEC*

Practice Questions

Q1   Briefly explain the term "fringe benefits".

Q2   List and explain three non-financial motivators.

Q3   Suggest three ways in which a workforce might benefit from change.

Q4   How might a strong leader make change easier for his or her employees to deal with?

Exam Questions

Q1   To what extent are the theories of the motivational theorists still useful for managers of modern companies?   (10 marks)

Q2   Greens of Snowbridge are hoping to open a new production plant for packaging their peas. They need to decide how to pay their staff. Discuss which financial incentives might best motivate their new staff.   (8 marks)

I wonder if hairdressers get fringe benefits...

So, there are lots and lots of ways of motivating people, but it's worth starting by learning that they can be roughly divided into two different categories — financial and non-financial. Remember too that people generally like having more responsibility — I guess it stops them getting bored and staring out of the window all afternoon...

Leadership

Leadership has a huge effect on motivation. Most people work more effectively if they like their boss. Good leaders tend to have certain qualities in common, but they don't all manage in the same way. **For OCR, Edexcel and WJEC.**

Managers *often need to be* Leaders *as well*

1) Managers **set objectives** for their department, and for the people under them.
2) Managers **organise resources** to get the job done and **achieve** their objectives.
3) Leaders **motivate** people. They **inspire** people to do things which they wouldn't do otherwise.
4) Managers who are good leaders can **persuade** people that the decisions they make and the objectives they set are the **best** ones.

You could say that bosses get results from their employees by telling them what to do, whereas leaders get results through their employees by inspiring and supporting them.

Leaders *need good* Leadership Qualities

Leaders tend to have a few **important characteristics** in common:

1) Leaders are **good at analysis**, and they can easily **spot a problem** and see potential **solutions**.
2) They **get on with people** at all levels and they're excellent **communicators**.
3) Leaders believe in their own **abilities**, but they can also identify their **weaknesses**.
4) Leaders see the **bigger picture** and are good at **persuading** others to **share** their view.
5) Their solutions to problems and their methods are **creative** and **imaginative**.
6) Leaders can act **strongly** and **decisively** when they need to.

There are various different Management Styles

1) The **authoritarian** or **autocratic** style — the **manager makes decisions** on his or her own. They identify the objectives of the business and say how they're going to be achieved. This style is useful when dealing with lots of **unskilled** workers, and in crisis management. It requires lots of **supervision** and monitoring — workers can't make their own decisions. An authoritarian style can **demotivate** able and intelligent workers.

2) The **paternalistic** (fatherly) style is a softer form of the autocratic style. The manager makes the decisions after **consultation** with others. They **explain** their decisions to the workers in an attempt to **persuade** the employees that such decisions are in everyone's interest. Paternalistic managers think that getting **involved** and caring about human relations is a **positive motivator**.

3) The **democratic** style — managers encourage the workforce to **participate** in the decision-making process. They **discuss** issues with workers, **delegate responsibility** and **listen** to advice. Democratic leaders have to be good communicators, and their organisations have to be good at dealing with loads of **to-and-fro communication**. This management style shows managers have a lot of confidence in the workforce — which leads to increased employee **motivation**. It also takes some of the **weight** of decision-making off the manager.

The best leaders are the ones who can adapt their style to suit the situation. It's hard to adapt like that, and most leaders have their own natural style that they're happiest with.

4) The **laissez-faire** style is a weak form of leadership. **Management rarely interferes** in the running of the business and the workforce is left to get on with trying to achieve the objectives of the business with minimal input and control from the top. This **hands-off** style of leadership might be appropriate for a small, highly motivated team of **able** workers. For workers who need guidance, it'd be a bit of a disaster.

Leadership

Various Factors affect which Management Style is most Appropriate

1) The way the organisation's been run in the past affects the **expectations** of the workforce, which affects how they might respond to leadership.

2) A **large**, **unskilled** workforce suits an **authoritarian** leadership style, whereas a **small**, **educated** workforce suits a **democratic** approach better.

3) **Urgent** tasks need different management and leadership from **routine** tasks.

4) The **best** type of **leader** is someone who is capable of **switching** from one **leadership style** to another depending on **what** is happening and **who** they are dealing with.

McGregor's Theory X and Theory Y of management — are workers lazy?

Douglas McGregor looked at management styles in big corporations. He believed managers fell into one of two categories — they were either **Theory X** or **Theory Y** managers.

Beliefs of Theory X Managers	Beliefs of Theory Y Managers
Workers don't like responsibility and are not ambitious.	Work comes naturally to most people — it's like eating or sleeping.
Workers need to be controlled. They will only make an effort if they are closely supervised.	Most employees are creative and imaginative and these skills should be put to use.
Workers value security more than anything else.	Given the chance, workers will look for responsibility.
A typical employee dislikes work and will avoid it if possible.	Supervision and punishment are not the only ways of motivating people.

He's not essentially lazy — just poorly motivated.

1) McGregor thought **most** managers were Theory X managers. However, he went along with Theory Y himself.

2) Although McGregor used Theory Y, there are **times** when a **Theory X** approach might be **more suitable**. On the whole, if a situation calls for **autocratic** management, it could also be dealt with using Theory X.

3) **Theory Y** managers use methods that are **similar** to **Herzberg** and **Maslow's** theories of motivation (see p.54).

Practice Questions

Q1 In what ways do managers also need to be leaders?

Q2 Give three examples of good leadership qualities.

Q3 What is laissez-faire leadership?

Q4 Name two factors which affect a manager's choice of leadership style.

Q5 In what ways is a Theory X manager different from a Theory Y manager?

Exam Questions

Q1 Mr Fox is an authoritarian manager, whereas Mr White prefers the paternalistic style. Briefly explain how you would expect their styles of management to differ. (6 marks)

Q2 A supermarket manager wants to know which style of leadership he should use in order to motivate his checkout staff. Discuss which styles he should consider, giving your reasons. (12 marks)

I wanted to be a laissez-faire leader, but my workers don't speak French...

Leaders come in all shapes and sizes — there are the strict, mean ones who never stop cracking the whip, and the soft and cuddly kind who just want to be your friend. As it happens, both are capable of being good motivators — the best leaders will assess the situation in front of them and change their leadership style accordingly.

SECTION THREE — PEOPLE IN BUSINESS

Size and Efficiency

*When it comes to efficiency, productivity and unit costs, bigger is better — or so it seems. For **WJEC, OCR** and **Edexcel**.*

Operations Management is about Efficiency, Productivity and Quality

1) **Operations management** means managing a firm to produce **quality** goods with **low unit costs**, at the **right time**. Managers decide the right production methods, the right scale of production and the right amount of stock.

2) Good production **efficiency** means low costs per unit — there's a **balance** between **low costs** and **quality**.

3) In order to **monitor efficiency**, companies keep an eye on **turnover**, **profit** and employee **productivity**. There's more on how to **calculate** these on p.30 and 50.

4) Ideally, companies would **want** to achieve **maximum efficiency**. Some would like to operate on a large scale. In reality, they can only become as **big** and **efficient** as their **finances**, **technology** and **staff numbers** will allow.

5) **Productivity** measures **output** (number of items made) in terms of **input** (number of machines used, length of time a worker takes to make an item). It can be measured as **labour productivity**, e.g. **output per worker per day**, or as **capital productivity**, e.g. output per machine per week. It's related to the motivation stuff on p.54-57.

Economies of Scale mean bigger is Cheaper

Economies of scale mean that as **output increases**, the **cost** of producing **each item** goes down. **Internal** economies of scale increase efficiency **within** an individual firm. There are different types of internal economies of scale.

1) **Technical** economies of scale are all about **production**. Production methods for large volumes are often more **efficient**. Large businesses can afford to buy better, more advanced **machinery**, which means they might need fewer staff and wage costs will fall.

Even service sector industries can sometimes achieve technical economies of scale. They might save on wages by locating call centres abroad.

2) **Specialisation** economies of scale are to do with **employees**. Large businesses can employ managers with **specialist skills** and separate them out into specialised departments. This is **cheaper** than paying external firms to do the work.

3) **Purchasing** economies of scale are to do with **discounts**. Large businesses can negotiate **discounts** when **buying supplies**. They can get bigger discounts and longer credit periods than their smaller competitors.

4) **Financial** economies of scale are to do with **borrowing money**. Large firms can borrow at **lower rates of interest** than smaller firms. Lenders feel more comfortable lending money to a big firm than a small firm.

5) **Marketing** economies of scale are related to **promotion costs**. The cost of an ad campaign is a **fixed cost**. A business with a large output can share out the cost over more products than a business with a low output.

6) **Risk-bearing** economies of scale involve **diversification** into several different **markets** or to cater to several different **market segments**. Large firms have a greater ability to bear **risk** than their small competitors.

External Economies of Scale make a Whole Industry or Area more efficient

External economies of scale happen when industries are concentrated in small geographical areas.

1) Having an **established network of suppliers** gives economies of scale. Locating close together means firms can easily play local suppliers off against each other, which increases quality and reduces price.

2) A good skilled **labour supply** makes an industry more efficient. This is most important in industries where training is **expensive** or takes a long time. For example, software developers in California's "Silicon Valley" know that plenty of programmers who are qualified to fill their vacancies **already** live within driving distance.

3) Firms located in certain areas can benefit from good **infrastructure** — like an airport, a motorway or good rail links. E.g. Dublin's tourist industry had a massive boost in profits after Ryanair started **cheap flights** to Dublin.

Size and Efficiency

Diseconomies of Scale — being bigger can be Bad News, too

Diseconomies of scale make unit costs of production rise as output rises. They happen because large firms are harder to manage than small ones. They're caused by poor **motivation**, poor **communication** and poor **coordination**.

1) In a big firm, it's hard to **coordinate** activities between different departments. It's important to keep all departments working towards the **same objectives**. Poor coordination makes a business **drift off course**.

2) **Communication** is harder in a big business. It can be **slow** and **difficult** to get messages to the right people, especially when there are **long chains of command**. The **amount** of information circulating in a business can increase at a faster rate than the business is actually growing.

3) It can be hard to **motivate** people in a large company. In a **small** firm, managers are in **close contact** with staff, and it's easier for people to feel like they **belong** and that they're working towards the same aims. When people **don't feel they belong**, and that there's **no point** to what they're doing, they get **demotivated**.

4) Diseconomies of scale are caused by problems with management. Strong **leadership**, **delegation** and **decentralisation** can all help **prevent diseconomies** of scale and keep costs down.

5) It's much **easier** to measure and quantify **economies** of scale than **diseconomies** of scale. For example, it's **easy** to calculate the **cost** of a new piece of machinery and work out its **cost per unit** for different levels of output. But, it's **hard** to work out exactly how **motivated** employees will be at different levels of output or how bad **communication problems** will be at various output levels.

Businesses have to Choose the Right Scale of production

1) A business needs to get **output** to levels where **economies of scale** make **unit costs** as **low** as possible — without letting **diseconomies of scale** start pushing unit costs up again.

2) Ideally, a firm would want the **bottom** of the **curve** on the graph to be as far to the **right** as possible. It's better for a firm to output 500 units at £5 per unit than 200 units, because this keeps costs down. The further the **base** of the **curve** is to the **right**, the **more units** a business is able to produce at **low cost** without entering into diseconomies of scale.

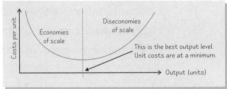

3) To make the base of the curve move right, a firm should **take advantage** of as many **economies of scale** as possible.

4) **Economies of scale** are one of the reasons it's **hard** for **small businesses** to compete with big ones. This is why small companies tend to cater for **niche**, instead of **mass**, markets (see p.79-80).

Growth helps a business Increase its Scale of production — WJEC

1) **Organic** (internal) **growth** happens **within** the company, e.g by moving into foreign markets. It tends to be **slow**.

2) **External** growth involves **mergers** or **acquisitions**. A **merger** is when two firms **agree** to **join together**, while an **acquisition** means one firm **taking control** of another firm by buying at least 50% of its share capital. This type of growth is **rapid** but can cause **managerial problems**.

3) A firm can **merge** with another company at the **same stage** of production (**horizontal integration**) or with a firm at a **different stage** of production (**vertical integration**). If **two** fish finger **manufacturers** merge, it's **horizontal** integration, but if a fish **supplier** merges with a fish **packaging company**, it's **vertical** integration.

— WJEC — — WJEC —

Practice Questions

Q1 Identify three benefits that firms would hope to get by increasing their size.

Q2 Give an example of a diseconomy of scale.

Q3 Which are easiest to measure, economies of scale or diseconomies of scale? Explain your answer.

Exam Questions

Q1 Discuss the economies of scale that will be of most benefit to a large manufacturing firm such as Dyson. (4 marks)

Q2 To what extent should a business accept diseconomies of scale as inevitable? (6 marks)

So it isn't what you do with it — it's how big it is that counts...

If you remember anything from these pages, remember "bigger is cheaper, but too big and you've got problems". If you want to get the marks for analysis and evaluation, you'd be well advised to learn the various ways that economies of scale can happen. That way you can mould the idea of economy of scale to the particular situation given in an exam question.

Capacity Utilisation

Changes in capacity utilisation impact on a company's break-even point and profit levels. **For all four boards.**

Capacity is Maximum Output with the Resources Currently Available

1) The **capacity** of an organisation is the **maximum** output that it can produce in a given period without buying any more fixed assets — machinery, factory space, etc.

2) Capacity depends on the **number of employees** and how skilled they are.

3) Capacity depends on the kind of production **process** the business uses.

4) Capacity depends on **technology** — what **machinery** and **computer systems** a business has and the state it's in.

5) The amount of **investment** in the business is also a factor.

Capacity Utilisation is How Much Capacity is being Used

$$\text{Capacity Utilisation} = \frac{\text{Output}}{\text{Capacity}} \times 100\%$$

Capacity utilisation depends on demand.

For example: a hotel with half its rooms booked out has a capacity utilisation of 50%. A clothing factory with an output of 70 000 shirts per month and a maximum capacity of 100 000 shirts is running at 70% capacity utilisation.

Under-utilisation is Inefficient and increases Unit Costs

Low capacity utilisation is called **under-utilisation**. It's **inefficient** because it means a business is **not getting use out of machines and facilities** that have been paid for.

1) Under-utilisation increases costs because **fixed costs** are **spread** over less **output**, so unit costs increase.

2) Higher capacity utilisation creates **economies of scale** (see p.60), which means a decrease in variable costs.

3) Operating under-capacity in the **long term** can cause firms to make **big losses** and **force** them to **rationalise**.

$$\text{Unit costs} = \text{total costs} \div \text{output}$$

You'll need to know how to calculate this in the exam.

Example: A chocolate factory's total costs are £7200 a month. In June, output was 18 000 chocolate bars, giving a unit cost of £0.40. In July, absenteeism caused output to fall to 16 000 bars, and the unit cost rose to £0.45.

90% Capacity Utilisation can be better than 100% Capacity Utilisation

High capacity utilisation is better than low capacity utilisation. However, 100% capacity utilisation has drawbacks.

1) Businesses have to consider all their **operational targets** when they plan their capacity usage. **Cost** isn't the only thing to think about — it might not be possible to operate at 100% capacity and keep **quality** levels high.

2) The business may have to turn away potential **customers**.

3) There's no **downtime** — machines are on **all the time**. If a machine has a problem, it'll cause delays and bottlenecks as work piles up waiting for the problem to be fixed. There's no time for equipment maintenance, which can reduce the life of machinery.

Businesses should plan production levels to achieve almost full capacity utilisation.

4) There's no **margin of error**. Everything has to be perfect first time, which causes **stress** to managers. **Mistakes** are more likely when everyone's working flat out.

5) The business can't **temporarily increase output** for seasonal demand or one-off orders.

6) If output is greater than demand, there'll be **surplus stock** hanging about waiting to be sold. It's not good to have valuable **working capital** tied up in stock.

Capacity utilisation can be Increased by Reducing Capacity

1) If a business is **operating under capacity** and they think that demand isn't going to go up in the future, they need to **reduce their capacity**. This is called **rationalisation** (or **downsizing**). It's popular with large firms who want to stay competitive by cutting their production costs.

2) Businesses can reduce capacity in the **short term** by stopping **overtime** or reducing the length of the working week, allocating staff to **other work** in the business, and by not renewing **temporary contracts**.

3) Businesses can reduce capacity in the **long term** by not **replacing** staff as they retire (natural wastage), making staff **redundant**, and by **selling off** factories or equipment.

4) An area of work with low capacity utilisation can be **sub-contracted out** to a specialist firm (see p.63).

Capacity Utilisation

Over Capacity production means firms need More Staff working More Often

If a firm is operating near to full capacity and has a sudden increase in demand, there are methods it can use to allow it to **operate** at **over 100% capacity** for a **short** period of time.

1) Businesses can use their facilities for **more** of the **working week**. They can have staff working in **shifts** or working **overtime** on weekends and bank holidays. They can also employ **temporary** or **part-time staff**.

2) Businesses can also increase their capacity utilisation by increasing **productivity**. They can reorganise production by reallocating staff to the busiest areas of the company. In the long term, they might try to improve productivity by increasing staff **motivation**.

3) It's also possible for businesses to **sub-contract** work to other businesses in **busy periods**. **Sub-contracting** is when a business uses its **facilities** to do work on behalf of **another business**. For example, a manufacturer of washing powder might make washing powder for a **supermarket** and package it with the supermarket's own label. The **advantage** of sub-contracting excess work is that it allows firms to respond to **unexpected increases in demand** without having the costs of extra staff and facilities all year round.

4) If the increased **demand** is expected to last a **long time**, firms might consider **recruiting** new staff. **Permanent** staff are **cheaper** than temporary workers in the long run.

Businesses Change capacity utilisation to match Predicted Demand

It's pointless producing more than you can sell, so companies alter capacity utilisation depending on demand.

1) Demand **changes** over time, so firms must think about demand in the **future** as well as the current demand.

2) The key to **long-term** success is planning **capacity** changes to match long-term changes in demand. Market research helps predict future demand, but it's not 100% certain. There's always an element of risk.

3) Firms should be flexible and **temporarily** increase capacity utilisation if an increase in demand isn't expected to continue in the **long term** — for example, with seasonal products like Christmas crackers, products heading towards decline in their life cycle, and one-off special orders.

4) **Long-term** solutions end up giving **lower unit costs** — as long as **predictions** of demand turn out to be **true**.

Some things get more demanding as they reach the end of their life cycle.

Practice Questions

Q1 Calculate capacity utilisation for a restaurant that has 65 seats but only 42 people dining each night.

Q2 Calculate how much it costs to produce one shirt, if a factory is making 450 shirts a month and has total monthly costs of £1600.

Answers for these two on p.108.

Q3 Explain what is meant by "rationalisation".

Exam Questions

Q1 Discuss why 95% capacity utilisation is considered better for a firm than 100%. (4 marks)

Q2 Analyse how a manufacturer of fashion clothing should expand their business if recent growth has led to capacity utilisation reaching 100%. (10 marks)

She cannae take any more, Jim...

Capacity utilisation crops up elsewhere. Under-utilisation is a consequence of low demand. When a business launches a product, capacity utilisation starts out low and then builds up as demand for the new product increases. You'd better learn how businesses get their capacity utilisation to round about 90% or so. It doesn't just happen by chance, that's for sure.

Types of Production

There are several ways of organising production — the key difference is between lovingly handcrafting every item, or cranking identical products out of a machine. **These two pages are for OCR, WJEC and Edexcel.**

Job Production is One-off production

1) Job production produces unique products or services. Each item is finished before the next item is started.

2) Job production is **labour-intensive**, using skilled workers. It has a high **labour to capital ratio** — i.e. it uses a lot of labour and doesn't need much capital investment.

3) It produces **small quantities**, often **made to order**. Products can be **tailored** to customer requirements.

4) Examples include hairdressing, and making wedding dresses, hand-made cards, jewellery and original paintings.

Advantages of Job Production	Disadvantages of Job Production
High **quality** products, specific to customer requirements.	Skilled labour is **expensive**.
High **added value**, so even low sales can make a profit.	Low output means **no economies of scale**.
Good **customer service** helps the business get repeat sales.	It takes **time** to make products to order — there are **no impulse purchases**. Customers go elsewhere for instant service.
Set-up costs are **low** — big machines aren't used.	There's **low capacity utilisation** of **equipment** — skilled workers use a variety of tools rather than one tool all the time.

Batch Production makes Identical Batches of product

1) Products pass through each stage of the production process in **batches**.

2) All items in a batch are **identical** but changes can be made between batches. It's a **compromise** between **job** and **flow** production.

3) Batches of **different components** can be made on the **same machine** using batch production and then put together in a separate operation. E.g. a machine dyes a batch of 5000 pieces of leather red in week 1 and makes a batch of 5000 plastic soles in week 2. Then in week 3 it assembles the two parts together to make shoes.

Advantages of Batch Production	Disadvantages of Batch Production
Lower unit costs than with **job** production.	**Higher** unit costs than with **flow** production.
Output is **higher** than with job production.	It takes **time** to **retool** machines to make a different batch.
Batch production is **flexible**.	Batch production needs careful **planning** and **coordination**.
Lots of **different components** can be made with **one machine**, which helps save costs.	There can be **high** levels of **work in progress**. One batch can sit around until another batch is finished before assembly.

Flow Production is Mass production on an Assembly Line

Flow production is sometimes called continuous production.

1) Flow production is a **continuous** process where products are assembled in a series of stages. It's used to make a large volume of identical, **standardised** products.

2) Flow production often uses a **production line** where components pass along a **conveyor belt**. At each stage of the process, a worker does a **set task** as the components pass by. They do the same task all day so they don't have to be skilled. Car assembly lines are a good example.

3) Flow production has **high set-up costs** — production-line machines are **expensive**. Flow production is **capital intensive**, and has a **low** labour to capital ratio.

4) Flow production needs **high-volume sales** to reach **break-even** point — because the **fixed costs** of machinery are so high. It isn't suitable for low demand, or for demand that goes up and down a lot.

Advantages of Flow Production	Disadvantages of Flow Production
Low unit costs due to economies of scale.	High **start-up costs**.
Production is **fast** and **efficient**.	Needs **constant, predictable demand**.
Low levels of **work in progress**, so doesn't need much storage space.	Flow production needs careful **planning** to avoid hold-ups. The whole process has to keep moving all the time.

Different Production methods have Different effects on Efficiency

1) **Job production** is relatively **inefficient** because each unit takes a worker a long time to make, although goods made in this way might sell at higher prices because they are unique.

2) **Batch production** and **flow production** have **greater production** and **labour efficiency** than job production.

Types of Production

Several *Factors Affect* the choice of *Production Method*

1) **Customer requirements**. Firms whose customers want unique and tailor-made goods will use job production. When customers demand low prices and accept standardised products businesses will use flow production.

2) **Demand**. Flow production is only possible with **high** and **unchanging demand**. Batch production may be more suitable if customers want some choice.

3) **Resources**. Firms with a pool of highly skilled labour will naturally be good at job production and are likely to experience poor motivation if they try to move away from this. A business without enough finance wouldn't be able to introduce flow production even if they wanted to.

4) The **aims and objectives** of the business. An objective of **maximising productivity** and **profit** goes with **flow** production. An objective of building a **personal relationship** with a customer goes with **job production**.

You have to *Balance Labour* vs *Capital* and *Flexibility* vs *Productivity*

Labour vs Capital

1) Job production is **labour-intensive**, but doesn't need much **capital**. It has a high labour to capital ratio.

2) Flow production is **capital-intensive**, but doesn't require much **skilled labour**. It has a low labour to capital ratio.

3) Technological advances make it possible for flow production to use **industrial robots** instead of human workers. Industrial robots are very **expensive**, and because they replace human workers they make the **labour to capital ratio** even **lower** than for traditional assembly line production.

Flexibility vs Productivity

1) Job production is **very flexible**, but it only produces small amounts of product per worker.

2) Flow production is **inflexible**, but produces huge amounts of product per worker.

3) Batch production is fairly **flexible**.

Businesses need *Physical Resources* to produce goods — *WJEC*

1) **Physical resources** are the things that a business **needs** to **produce goods** (apart from its staff). In other words, **land**, **machinery**, **raw materials**, **vehicles** and other **equipment**.

2) It's worth remembering that **land** isn't just used as somewhere to build a **factory** or a **warehouse**. It can also be **used** as a **raw material** (if it's agricultural land, or a mine, for example).

See p.47 for more on depreciation.

3) Physical resources have a big **effect** on a company's **finances**. The **price** of resources can **rise or fall**, which affects how much **capital** is **available** to the business. Machinery and vehicles lose value through **depreciation**.

4) Businesses also need to make sure they keep up with **advances** in **technology**. If a **competitor** buys a brand **new machine**, they may well become **more efficient**.

— WJEC — *WJEC*

Practice Questions

Q1 Describe the main differences between job, batch and flow production in terms of set-up costs, unit costs, product variety and output.

Q2 Suggest three disadvantages of using the flow production method.

Q3 State four factors to consider when choosing a method of production.

Exam Questions

Q1 Why might the exclusive sports car manufacturer TVR use job production when Ford uses flow production? (8 marks)

Q2 Why might flow production increase productivity in the short term then reduce it in the longer term? (8 marks)

I'm not going to make the obvious gag about bakers...

As far as basic facts go, you sort this lot out into three main headings — job production, flow production and batch production. You have to know the facts about what they are, how much they cost to set up, how efficient they are, etc. You also need to be able to evaluate which method might be suitable for a given business. Then go and put the kettle on.

Producing Quality Products

*Increased competition means firms now compete through quality as well as price. High quality increases revenues and reduces costs. Sounds like a good thing. **These pages are for AQA, WJEC, OCR and Edexcel.***

Good Quality products and services Meet Customer Needs

1) Products have to be **fit** for the **purpose** they're made for. For example, the quality of a tin-opener is judged by how well it opens tins.

2) The **customer's opinion** of quality is the most important one. Businesses should use **market research** to check customers are satisfied with product quality.

Hannah thought her skirt was quality, and that was all that really mattered.

Quality Control and Quality Assurance are Different Things

Quality control means **detecting** mistakes — **checking** goods for **faults** or **poor quality**.
Quality assurance means **preventing** mistakes — **designing** the production process so **faults don't happen**.

1) The traditional quality control approach assumes that errors are **unavoidable**. It says that the best you can do is to **detect errors** and **put them right** before customers buy the products.

2) Traditionally, **quality control inspectors** checked other people's work. This has drawbacks — inspectors are additional staff and need to be paid, and employees feel distrusted and demotivated.

3) Thinking that errors and faults are inevitable gives the production department the idea that they **needn't bother** to avoid mistakes. The quality control inspectors will always pick up mistakes later.

4) With modern approaches to quality control, workers check their own work. This is called **self-checking**. **Empowering** employees to check the quality of their own work can be highly **motivating**.

5) Under a quality assurance system, it's **everyone's responsibility** to produce good work. Everyone should try to get it **right first time**. Workers can **reject** components or work in progress if they're not up to standard. They don't pass the poor quality off as **someone else's problem**. Workers are responsible for passing on good quality work in progress to the next stage of the production process.

6) **Training** is really important for quality assurance. Workers are trained to produce good quality products and services. New recruits get this as part of **induction**. Experienced workers might need **retraining** from time to time.

7) Workers must be **motivated** and **committed** to quality for quality assurance schemes to work.

8) Quality assurance also depends on using **quality suppliers**. If the raw materials are no good, it's impossible to produce quality goods.

9) The ultimate aim of quality assurance is to create a culture of **zero defects**.

Quality, motivation and training are linked.

Quality Awards are Evidence of High Standards

1) **BS 5750** is an award given out by the **British Standards Institution** to firms with good quality assurance systems which meet the industry standard. **ISO 9000** is the **European** quality award. It's equivalent to BS 5750.

2) To get the award, a business must set **quality targets**, make sure their production process **achieves** these targets, and **monitor** production quality. This can **cost money**.

3) The British Standards Institution **doesn't care** too much what the business' quality assurance systems actually are, only that the business has systems in place to meet its own targets.

There are Laws to Protect Customers ——— *Edexcel only*

1) There are laws in place to ensure that businesses produce **goods** of a **minimum standard** — they have to be **fit for purpose** (which basically means they can do whatever it is that the manufacturer claims they can do).

2) Companies also have to make sure their product will **not harm** the customer and that the information on the **packaging** is **not misleading**. There's also a law which says they have to **reply** to customer **complaints**.

3) It can be **expensive** for companies to make sure their product meets all these laws, but if they didn't, it's very likely that the company would face **legal action** and serious **damage** to their **reputation**.

Edexcel only

Edexcel only

Producing Quality Products

There are **Several Approaches** to **Quality Assurance**

Total Quality Management is the ultimate, extreme version of Quality Assurance

1) **Total Quality Management** (TQM) means the **whole workforce** has to be committed to quality improvements. The idea is to **build quality** into every department and not let quality get squeezed out.

2) With TQM, every employee has to try to **satisfy customers** — both **external** customers that the business sells things to, and **internal** customers within the business.

3) It takes **time** to introduce TQM. Employees can be **demotivated** — TQM can seem like a lot of extra work. Workers need **training** so that they see quality as their responsibility. **Rewards** for quality can be motivating.

Benchmarking looks for top quality in other businesses, and learns from their example

1) **Benchmarking** means studying **other businesses** with excellent **quality standards**, and **adopting** their **methods**.

2) Benchmarking isn't always appropriate. **Competitors** are unlikely to **share** important information, and **working practices** can't always be transferred between different **corporate cultures** if firms don't operate in a similar way.

Quality circles are groups of employees who work on quality issues

1) **Quality circles** include employees from **various departments**. They meet to **identify** and **solve** problems.

2) Quality circles can be very effective at raising quality because they use the **knowledge** and **expertise** of factory floor staff — as long as staff are **motivated** by the initiative to share their thoughts and suggestions.

High Quality Increases Profits

Quality improvements reduce costs:

1) Fewer **raw materials** and less **worker** and **machinery** time get used up by **mistakes**.

2) You don't need as much **advertising** and **promotional** gubbins to persuade **shops** to stock high quality goods.

3) You don't need to spend as much on **marketing** to attract **new customers**.

4) You need fewer **customer care staff** because there aren't as many **complaints** to deal with.

5) There are fewer **refunds** and fewer claims on **warranties**.

Quality improvements increase revenue:

1) You don't need to **discount** prices to sell **damaged stock** when there isn't any damaged or "seconds" quality stock.

2) You can **charge more** — high quality products allow for **premium pricing**.

3) High quality products improve the **image** and **reputation** of the business.

4) Quality goods and services make it easy to keep **existing customers**.

5) A good reputation for quality brings in **new customers**.

> High quality products give businesses more flexibility when it comes to price. They can also use quality as a unique selling point (USP).

Practice Questions

Q1   Explain what is meant by a "quality product".

Q2   What's the difference between quality control and quality assurance?

Q3   Explain the concept of TQM.

Exam Questions

Q1   Examine the potential costs and benefits of obtaining ISO 9000 certification.   (8 marks)

Q2   The Managing Director of Bling Textiles decides to introduce Total Quality Management to the business. Explain why employees may be resistant to TQM, and suggest how it might be successfully introduced.   (10 marks)

AS Examiners — the ultimate quality control inspectors...

It's pretty obvious that good quality is important in business. People don't like paying for things that aren't any good. There are different ways to go about making sure that products and services are of good quality — one important difference is between quality control inspections of finished products and quality assurance systems for the whole production process.

Stock Control

Good stock management is a balance between keeping stocks as low as possible, to save money, and avoiding running out of stock, causing inconvenience to customers and losing revenue. **These pages are for WJEC, OCR and Edexcel.**

Businesses need *Stock* — *Materials*, *Work in Progress* and *Finished Items*

1) **Raw materials**, **work in progress** and **finished items** are all types of **stock**.

2) **Raw materials** are all the things needed in the production of an item. Businesses **need** raw materials in stock so that machines and workers don't sit **idle** waiting for raw materials to arrive.

3) **Work in progress** (or **WIP** for short) are items part-way through the production process.

4) **Finished products** are complete items in the warehouse that haven't been **sold** yet. Finished stock is there to satisfy customer demand **instantly**.

5) Businesses need stock to **keep production going** and to cope with customer **demand**. Businesses without enough raw materials can't produce finished goods. Businesses without enough finished goods in stock can't respond to sudden customer demand.

It's *Costly* to hold lots of *Stock*

1) **Storage costs** are the most **obvious cost** of holding stock. Storage costs include rent for the warehouse and also the non-obvious costs of heating, lighting, refrigeration, security etc. Don't forget those.

2) **Wastage costs** are the costs of **throwing away** useless stock. The longer a business holds stock, the more likely it is to create waste. Stocks get **physically damaged** as time goes on, and they can also go **out of fashion**.

3) **Opportunity cost** (see p.31) is the cost of **investing** money in stock instead of **something else**. Capital tied up in stock is **unproductive**, affects **cash flow** and could be used more productively elsewhere, such as financing a marketing campaign.

The value of stock a business is holding is recorded on the **balance sheet** (see p.46 - 47), and features in the trading part of the **profit and loss account** (as opening and closing stock — see p.44).

Buffer Stock is the *Minimum* amount of stock a *Business Needs*

A business needs a **minimum** level of stock so it **won't run out** of materials or finished goods. Running out of **raw materials** or **work in progress** means that production grinds to a **halt** — very bad news. Running out of a **product** means that customers have to be **turned away** — more bad news. The minimum stock level is called the **buffer stock**.

1) The level of buffer stock depends on the **warehouse space** available.

2) Buffer stock levels also depend on the **kind** of product you're storing — a **perishable** food item will have lower buffer stock levels than something which keeps, to reduce the risk of it **going off**.

3) The level of buffer stock depends on the **rate** at which the business **uses up** its stocks. If it goes through stocks like a knife through butter, it'll need to hold more stock.

4) **Suppliers** are a massive factor in working out buffer stock levels. The **lead time** is the time it takes for goods to **arrive** after ordering them from the supplier. The **longer** the lead time, the **more buffer stocks** you need to hold — if customer demand suddenly went up, you wouldn't want to wait a long time for stocks to arrive from the supplier. A **short lead time** means you can have **small** buffer stocks and top them up as and when you need to.

Stock, stock, lovely stock. Piles and piles of beautiful stock...

Just-in-time production takes short lead times to the extreme (see p.70 for more on JIT).

Stock Control

Stock Control Charts help control Stock Management

Stock control charts allow managers to **analyse** and **control** stock over a period of time — as shown below. Have a good look at the diagram. It'll make stock control easier to understand. If you're doing **OCR** or **Edexcel**, you can be asked to **analyse** (and **draw** — **OCR** only) a stock control chart, too.

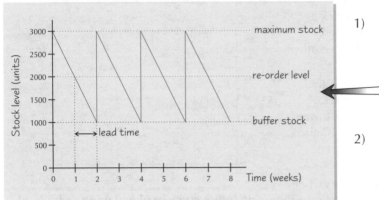

1) The **buffer stock level** is **1000 units**. The **lead time** is 1 week, and the business goes through **1000 units** each week. That means they have to **re-order** stock when they've got **2000** units left — just so they don't go below their buffer stock level. 2000 units is the **re-order level**. (Catchy name, huh.)

2) The business re-orders **2000 units** of stock each time. This takes them back up to their **maximum stock level** of 3000 units.

1) In this chart, the **buffer stock** level, **lead time** and **re-order** level are all the **same** as in the graph above.

2) However, in this graph **usage increases** by **200%** between weeks 6 and 7. This means the company uses **3000 units** in **one week**, causing it to **run out** of **stock**.

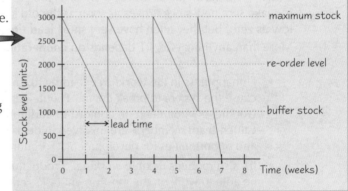

3) Businesses can **improve stock control** by improving their **supply chain** (introducing better computer systems, for example), being on **good terms** with their **suppliers**, and ensuring that they have identified any **seasonal peaks** in demand.

Stock Rotation has to go in the right sequence — First In, First Out

1) Stock rotation means **arranging** stock so it's **used** in the order it was **purchased**.

2) Employees re-stocking products put the **new** items at the **back** of the shelf so they're used last. This is called "**first in, first out**" or FIFO for short.

3) If they put new stock at the front of the shelf, the stock at the back may **never** be used until it's **out of date**. This isn't such bad news for rolls of cloth, but it's disastrous for pints of milk.

Practice Questions

Q1 Define the three types of stock a business might hold.

Q2 Describe the costs associated with holding high stocks.

Q3 Explain what is meant by "buffer stock".

Q4 Give three examples of ways in which businesses can improve their stock control.

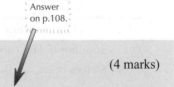

Answer on p.108.

Exam Questions

Q1 James Cook runs a fish and chip shop. Suggest whether he should keep a high or low level of buffer stock, and explain your reasons. (4 marks)

Q2 Draw a stock control chart for a car salesman who sells 45 cars a week, with a re-order level of 25 units, a buffer stock level of 10 cars, and a maximum stock level of 55 units. (4 marks)

Do gravy manufacturers have minimum stock levels...

It's important to have the right level of stock. Too much, and you're paying to have stock sitting around for no reason, and tying up cash for no reason. Too little, and production will grind to a halt, or customers will stalk out of the shop in disgust because you've run out of ice lollies on the hottest day of the year. Also, you need good stock to make good soup.

Increasing Efficiency

Lean production is all about stamping out wasteful habits and turning the business into one lean, mean, making-things machine. It's actually worth having a gander at the pages on stock (p.68-69) as well, cos it's all part of a glorious interconnected web of operational efficiency. **These pages are for all four boards — AQA, Edexcel, OCR and WJEC.**

Just-in-Time (JIT) reduces *Costs* but needs *Very Effective Management*

1) **Just-in-time (JIT)** production aims to have as little **stock** as possible — ideally, raw materials come in one door, are made into products and go straight out another door — all **just in time** for delivery to customers.

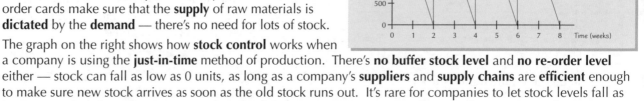

2) JIT is based on very efficient **stock control**. **Kanban** is the name given to the system used to **trigger repeat orders**. When employees reach coloured kanban order cards towards the end of a batch of components, they order more. Kanban order cards make sure that the **supply** of raw materials is **dictated** by the **demand** — there's no need for lots of stock.

3) The graph on the right shows how **stock control** works when a company is using the **just-in-time** method of production. There's **no buffer stock level** and **no re-order level** either — stock can fall as low as 0 units, as long as a company's **suppliers** and **supply chains** are **efficient** enough to make sure new stock arrives as soon as the old stock runs out. It's rare for companies to let stock levels fall as low as zero, but they often have very **short lead times** (see p.68). **Supermarkets** tend to operate in this way.

4) More than anything else, JIT depends on **cooperation**:

- Unhappiness in the **workforce** leading to low productivity, absenteeism (sickies) or strikes will cause the system to break down. **People-centred management** can help to create a satisfying working environment. In contrast to traditional management approaches, workers are treated as valued **team members**, are involved in decision-making, and are given increased responsibility and opportunities for development. For more on management, see p.58-59.

- JIT also requires **flexible working**. Production is tied to customer **demand**, so **employees** need to be able to work on the most urgent tasks, **coordinating** their efforts to keep production moving. This is different from traditional repetitive factory work, and fits in nicely with people-centred management.

- Slow or unreliable deliveries from **suppliers** will make JIT production unworkable. Businesses using JIT usually have links and long-term partnerships with suppliers.

Just-in-Time *makes companies* Flexible, *but can be* Risky

Benefits of just-in-time production:

1) The cost of **storage space** (e.g. **rent**) for materials, work in progress and finished goods is reduced.

2) **Cash flow** is improved — working capital isn't tied up in work in progress.

3) **Productivity** is higher — JIT uses less material, space, time and money to get the same output.

4) There's greater **flexibility** because products are built to order.

5) There's **less waste** — there's no old, damaged or out-of-date stock lying around.

Drawbacks of just-in-time production:

1) **Supplier delays** can cause production to **stop** immediately. There's no stock to keep things going.

2) **Strikes** bring **supply** to a halt. There's no **finished stock** to supply customers when workers down tools.

3) Products have to be **perfect first time** — there isn't stock available to replace faulty products.

> Companies which use **just-in-time** production have very **short lead times**. This can give them a big **advantage** over their **competitors**, because it's **easier** for them to **respond** to **changes** in **demand**.

Increasing Efficiency

Lean Production aims to Reduce Costs by Cutting Out Waste

1) **Lean production** is a modern business philosophy based on the idea of increasing **efficiency** by cutting out all forms of **waste**, and really **streamlining** production.

2) Lean production tries to use less **time**, **space**, **raw materials** and **money**. Lean production is **more productive** than traditional mass production — it uses **less input** to get the **same output**.

3) Lean production techniques include **just-in-time** production (JIT), **cell** production, **continuous improvement** and **time-based management**.

4) **Kaizen**, or **continuous improvement**, is a Japanese idea. It's **similar** to the idea of **quality circles**, and involves groups of **workers** meeting regularly to **discuss improvements** to working practices. It's a good (and relatively cheap) way of making sure a **business** continues to **improve without** making **huge** and **expensive changes**.

5) **Training employees** for lean production costs money. Businesses need to take care that these costs don't outweigh the cost savings that they get from lean production.

The Advantages of Lean Production depend on Customers and Competitors

1) Lean producers tend to have **small volume** production runs and are more **flexible** than typical mass producers, who produce large quantities of identical products. This gives them an edge over mass producers when **product life cycles** are **short**, i.e. when fashions change quickly (see p.88-89). They benefit when customers demand more new, fashionable, "now" products — which they certainly seem to be doing these days...

2) Of course, the advantage a business gets from lean production depends on what **other businesses** are up to. If they've all got the lean production bug as well, it won't give as much of a **competitive advantage**.

Cell Production cuts out waste and Improves Motivation ——— OCR ———

1) Cell production divides production up into **self-contained teams** (cells) of employees. Each cell is responsible for one stage of the production process.

2) Workers in each team do a **range of tasks** to get the job done. They don't get stuck with one repetitive task all day, as with traditional assembly lines. Each cell is usually arranged in a **horseshoe** shape. Products circulate around the horseshoe, and then they're passed to the cell doing the next stage of the process.

3) Cells **self-check** the quality of the work they've done (see p.66), which helps cut out **mistakes**. The next cell along in the production process can send work back if it isn't right.

4) Because cells work on **small batches** of items, there's almost **no** work in progress. Work in progress is a form of **stock** — it takes up space and uses up working capital.

5) Workers **organise themselves** to perform whatever tasks are **necessary**. This helps with motivation — people like to organise themselves. It also avoids **bottlenecks** building up behind one slow worker.

6) The **teamworking** atmosphere and **job enrichment opportunities** that you get with cell production help improve employee motivation — which leads to even more productivity improvements.

——— OCR ——————————————— OCR ———

Practice Questions

Q1 What is meant by "kanban"?

Q2 State three benefits and three drawbacks of just-in-time production methods.

Q3 When do lean producers have an advantage over mass manufacturers?

Q4 Why might cell production improve employee motivation?

Exam Questions

Q1 What problems might a large manufacturer of skiing equipment experience when moving over to a just-in-time production system? (4 marks)

Q2 To what extent do you agree that all firms should use lean production methods? (10 marks)

Just-in-time — sometimes it just works, sometimes it just doesn't...

Lean production and just-in-time are great for cutting waste and making things efficient. They aren't always the be-all and end-all though, because they don't suit all businesses. If a business has flaky suppliers who don't deliver on time, just-in-time production will be a disaster. Cell production is a good way to motivate, avoid bottlenecks and improve quality.

Customer Service

Providing good customer service is one thing that makes businesses competitive in the long term. If a business is committed to providing good service, it needs to spend a lot of money and time developing a quality culture.
These pages are for AQA, Edexcel and WJEC.

Customers **Expect** good service from a **Company**

Basically, customer service means providing a service or product in the way that has been promised.

1) **Customer service** is the **actions** that a business takes to **keep** its **customers happy**. Customer service can be part of the sales process **before**, **during**, or **after** the sale itself.

2) Having a customer service **philosophy** means admitting to mistakes and dealing with complaints — customers like companies to admit when they're wrong, explain the problem and make amends. An important part of the process is making **customer service** part of the organisation's **culture**, and ensuring that all **employees** work hard to provide **excellent** levels of **customer service**.

3) Knowing the customer is **vital** to good customer service. A company has to know what its customers **want** and **expect** in order to be able to provide it — that's why **market research** (p.82-83) and **feedback** are so important. Companies can get feedback through guestbooks, questionnaires, **secret shoppers** (customers who are paid to use a service to provide feedback on it) and emails.

4) The way companies deliver customer service is **changing**. Email and chat systems make it easy for customers to speak to experts at **any time**, and call centres can handle **hundreds** of customers per hour. These developments have also made senior management more **directly involved** in customer services — in some cases (e.g. motorway service stations) you can directly telephone the **manager** to complain.

Good Customer Service gives companies a Competitive Advantage

Providing good customer service uses up **time** and **money**. There are plenty of reasons why many companies think it's still **worth** making the **effort**, though...

1) Good customer service can provide a **USP** (Unique Selling Point, see p.86).

2) Customers can now shop 24 hours a day, online or by phone, and expect to be able to buy products **quickly** and **easily**. Since many companies provide identical products at similar prices, most customers will go to one that offers high levels of **service** that are **consistently delivered**.

3) New products, services and technological improvements can be copied by the competition, but a good **service reputation** is **hard** to **duplicate**.

4) Companies that provide added value and superior customer service can **charge more** than their competitors.

5) **Long-term customers** buy more, take less company time, bring in new customers and are less **price sensitive** (put off by price rises). Companies now look at customers in terms of their **LTV** (Lifetime Value) to the company.

6) **Satisfied customers** are the best **advert** for the company as they spread its reputation by **word of mouth**.

In a world dominated by Chip and Pin technology, giving customers the chance to sign for goods was a unique customer service.

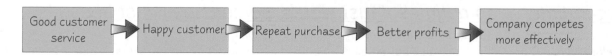

| Good customer service | Happy customer | Repeat purchase | Better profits | Company competes more effectively |

Customer Service

Different Types of Business offer Different Types of Customer Service

There are three basic factors that contribute to customer satisfaction:

1) Products and services need to be **customer-focused** and provide **value** for money.
2) Businesses have to treat customers as individuals with **different needs**.
3) **After-sales service** — following up with after-sales support such as maintenance.

Companies who want to get a **competitive advantage** from customer service often try to **go beyond** the types of service listed above. **How** they go about this depends on what type of business they are:

1) Businesses such as shops, where the customer comes **face to face** with staff, are likely to invest in **staff training**. **Extended opening hours** and **home delivery** might also improve customer satisfaction.
2) **Online** and **telephone retailers** don't deal with the customer face to face, so they have to find other ways of giving good customer service. Some have customer service **call centres** that are open **long hours**. Others offer **next-day** or **free delivery** or are more **flexible** about **returning** goods.
3) **Business to Business (B2B)** companies (see p.79) focus their customer service efforts on building **long-term relationships** with their **clients**, often by providing spare parts or maintenance. This is because businesses that sell to businesses usually have a **few clients** who each spend **lots** of **money**, whereas firms that sell to private customers have a lot of customers each spending relatively small amounts of money.

Research, Training and Quality Management all Improve Customer Service

Companies are always trying to monitor and improve the level of customer service that they offer. They do this by investing in market research and training and by introducing quality management systems.

1) **Market research** involves **gathering** and **analysing** information about customers through **customer surveys** and **questionnaires**. Managers can use this information to help them **understand** the **market** and make sure **products** and **services** meet the **customer's needs**. Look at pages 82-83 for more on market research.

Quality culture.

2) **Staff** should be **knowledgeable** about the product or service they are selling. Companies use **training** to make sure employees have this knowledge. Training can also be used to ensure that staff have a **positive attitude** towards the customer.

3) **Quality systems** ensure that products and services are **produced** and **sold** at an acceptable **standard** and **quality**. Firms can use methods of **quality assurance** such as **Total Quality Management** (TQM, see p.67) to create a quality culture and make sure all employees are contributing in some way to customer service targets. Alternatively, they might introduce **quality standards** such as ISO 9000 (See page 66).

Practice Questions

Q1 How would you define customer service?
Q2 Why is it beneficial for a company to have long-term customers?
Q3 What factors contribute to high levels of customer satisfaction?
Q4 How can a company benefit from satisfying customer needs?

Exam Question

Q1 (a) Discuss the alternatives a company has for developing its customer service. (10 marks)

(b) Evaluate the benefits it might gain as a result of improving its customer service. (6 marks)

All our writers are currently busy — please continue to hold...

When you've been waiting for someone to answer your call for an hour, it's easy to feel like companies don't care about customer service at all. But it costs them as much to win one new customer as it does to keep five existing ones. So, believe it or not, they're usually doing everything in their power to keep you sweet. Make sure you learn how they do it.

Suppliers

It's not called a supply chain for nothin' — every business in the chain needs to pull their weight, or production just doesn't happen... Plus, if you're lucky, suppliers might take you out for tea. **For AQA, Edexcel and WJEC.**

Producing **High Quality** products **Depends** on **Good Suppliers**

A company's **performance** is often **linked** to the activities and performance of its **suppliers**.

1) A **supply chain** consists of the group of **firms** that are involved in **all** the various **processes** required to make a **finished product / service** available to the customer.

2) The chain **begins** with the provider of **raw materials** and **ends** with the firm that sells the **finished product**.

3) The members of a supply chain will **vary** depending on the type of product/service, but will typically include **suppliers**, **manufacturers**, **distributors** and **retailers**.

4) **All** the **members** of the supply chain need to **function efficiently**. If any of them are unreliable, the product won't be on the shelves when it needs to be, or the quality will be poor, which reflects badly on the company producing it.

"We should be able to get those components to you by 1952."

Finding good **Suppliers** is the role of the **Purchasing Department**

Nearly all companies have a **purchasing department**. The purchasing department is responsible for **buying materials** (if the company is a manufacturer) or **stock** (if the company is a retailer).

1) **Efficient purchasing** is key to a firm's success. If the purchasing department in a factory is not functioning efficiently, the factory could run out of components and be forced to put **production** temporarily **on hold**. In retail, poor purchasing can lead to a **lack** of **stock** on the shelves or **too much** stock in the warehouse.

2) Effective purchasing departments consider **lots** of **factors** before choosing a **supplier**. See below for more about these factors.

WJEC — WJEC — WJEC — WJEC

Companies need to consider **Price** and **Reliability** when **Choosing a Supplier**

The most **effective suppliers** are those who offer products or services that **match** the **needs** of your business. So when you are looking for **suppliers**, it's best to be **sure** of your **business needs** and what you want to achieve. The most important factors to consider are:

Price	The **total cost** of acquiring the product. Firms have to decide **how much** they are willing to pay and whether **cost** is their **first priority**. If they want to cut down the time it takes to serve customers, suppliers that offer faster delivery will rate higher than those that compete on price alone.
Payment Terms	Companies need to know **how much** they need to pay, **how** it has to be paid and **when** it should be paid by. **Small suppliers** may only be able to offer **30 days' credit**, as they often have poor cash flow. Some **larger firms** may be able to offer as much as **120 days'** credit.
Quality	The **quality** of supplies needs to be **consistent** — customers associate **poor quality** with the business they buy from, not their suppliers.
Capacity	Businesses need to select **suppliers** who are able to **meet** any **peaks** in **demand** for particular products / services.
Reliability	If a **supplier** lets a **firm** down, that firm may not be able to supply its **own** customers. Suppliers need to **deliver on time**, or give plenty of **warning** if they can't.
Flexibility	**Suppliers** need to be able to **respond easily** to **changes** in a company's **requirements**. Efficient production relies on suppliers who can provide extra (or fewer) supplies at **short notice**.

Suppliers

Companies build **Relationships** with their **Suppliers**

A **strategic working relationship** is one where both companies in the relationship can get **long-term benefits** from **working together**. There are several ways for companies to build strategic working relationships with their suppliers:

1) **Linked Networks** — **shared IT systems** such as inventory (stock) control management allow both the company and its supplier to view stock levels, so they both know in plenty of time when more supplies will be needed. This can improve **efficiency**, cut **costs**, and improve **customer value**.

2) **JIT (Just-in-Time) Systems** — these are becoming a popular way of managing operations. The goal of JIT systems is to have only the **right amounts** of **materials** arrive at precisely the **times** they are **needed**. Because supplies arrive just as they are needed you don't need a big warehouse, and there's **less waste**. See p.70 for more on this.

3) **Shared Costs** — if a business and its supplier are producing similar goods, there's a good chance they'll be able to save money by sharing **specialist equipment** and storing their goods in the same **warehouse**.

A **Well-managed Supply Chain** can **Improve** operational **Performance**

If a business **works** closely with the **right suppliers**, there's a good chance that **operational performance** will **improve**. **Productivity** will **increase**, which causes **costs** to **fall** (for more on the link between these two, see p.50). Also, a business with an **efficient supply chain** is in a much better position to meet its customers' expectations.

1) A company's buyers need to make sure that they **only buy** the **supplies** that the **company** really **needs** — they mustn't be wowed by slick sales pitches.

2) They also need to understand the difference between a **strategic supplier**, who provides goods or services that are essential to the business — such as high-value raw materials — and a **non-strategic supplier**, who provides low-value supplies such as office stationery. It's important to spend **more time** selecting and managing **strategic suppliers** than non-strategic suppliers.

3) It's often easier, and generally more **cost-effective**, for businesses to **limit** the number of **sources** they buy from. However, it's **dangerous** to have just **one supplier** because if there are ever problems with that supplier, the business has nowhere to turn.

4) It's always worth having an **alternative supply source** ready to help in difficult times. This is really important for suppliers who are essential to the success of the business.

Mr MacDonald and Mr Paulin had spent three days choosing a supplier for a new stapler.

Practice Questions

Q1 What is meant by the term "supply chain?"
Q2 What factors should a firm consider when selecting a supplier?
Q3 Why would a business choose a JIT method of production?
Q4 What is the difference between a strategic supplier and a non-strategic supplier?

Exam Questions

Q1 Alpha Ironmonger Ltd. is looking for a supplier of beef to use in its new range of beef pies. Discuss the factors it should consider before deciding which one to choose. (8 marks)

Q2 Mr Brown, director of Browns Brushes Ltd, wants to improve his relationship with his suppliers. Discuss the ways in which he could go about achieving this. (8 marks)

Supply me to the moon — let me sing among the stock...

If you're a business, the relationship with your supplier might be the best one you'll ever have. Or the worst. If your suppliers do what they're supposed to when they're supposed to, there's a good chance that the production process will all run to plan. If they're late, or just don't deliver, production stops, staff have nothing to do — it's a disaster, basically...

Technology in Operations

Most modern businesses rely heavily on technology, from automated production lines to computer systems.
Technology can make a firm more cost-effective and efficient, but it needs constant updating and maintenance.
These pages are for AQA, OCR and WJEC.

Businesses use **Two** main types of **Technology**

The main technologies that companies use in day-to-day operations are:

1) **Robotic Engineering** — using robots as part of the manufacturing process.

2) **Computer Technology** — computers are used by businesses in lots of different ways. Product development, business communications and finance departments all depend on IT systems.

Using **Robots** can **Reduce Staffing Costs**

1) **Robots** are mostly used to replace human staff for **tasks** which are **dangerous**, **repetitive** or **boring**.

2) **Factories** and **production plants** often use **automated pickers** to take goods from the production line and pack them into boxes. It's usually **cheaper** and **faster** for robots to do this job instead of humans.

3) Companies that are planning to replace human workers with robots need to weigh up the **advantages** of using robots against the **demotivating effect** that it is likely to have on staff.

Advantages of using Robots	1) Company needs **fewer employees**, so staff **costs fall**. 2) Robots are generally more **accurate** — human error is eliminated. 3) Robots are more **reliable** than human workers. 4) Robots can be used for **tasks** that could be **unsafe** for **humans**, e.g. bomb detection.
Disadvantages of using Robots	1) Some **staff** may **lose their jobs**, which can be **demotivating** for colleagues. 2) **Incorrect programming** can lead to **errors** being made. 3) **High initial cost** involved in **purchasing** robot. 4) Maintenance costs can be **expensive**.

Luke claimed to be developing a new robot. His colleagues thought he was just playing chess.

IT helps make **Production** more **Efficient**

1) **Computer-aided design** (CAD) uses computers to design new products, or make alterations to existing products. CAD produces 3D mock-ups on screen — managers don't have to wait for a **prototype** (model) to be built before they know what the product will look like. This can also be useful for marketing things like new kitchens.

2) **Computer-aided manufacture** (CAM) uses computers to produce a product, usually involving **robots** or 'computer-numerically controlled' (**CNC**) machines — automatic lathes which form a material into a finished product from a computer design. CAM is often combined with the CAD process — products are designed on computer, and the design data fed straight into the production machine. This is called **CAD/CAM**.

3) Computers make **stock control** easier. Holding stock information in a database makes it much easier to monitor when you need to order new stock. In retailing this is often combined with **Electronic Point of Sale (EPOS)** systems that rely on barcodes to record which products are being purchased by customers. This means stocks can be re-ordered automatically. Having a good stock control system makes it easier for companies such as supermarkets and big retailers to move to a **just-in-time** supply system (see p.70).

IT helps make **Communication Faster** and more **Effective**

Communication now happens very **fast**, thanks to IT. Information can be shared **within** the **company** using an **intranet**. Businesses communicate with other **businesses** and with **customers** by **fax**, **email** and the **internet**.

1) Email is a fast and efficient method of communicating, both internally and externally.

2) The **internet** allows businesses to reach a **larger customer base**, and do business **24 hours a day**. Customers can check a **website** for information rather than phoning a helpline or sending a letter in the post.

IT helps make **Finance** departments more **Efficient**

1) **IT** helps with **budgetary control**. The finance department can easily compare current expenditure levels with original budgets using **spreadsheets**.

2) Spreadsheets allow managers to investigate "what if?" scenarios. They can calculate the impact of **potential changes** in expenditure or sales, which makes **decision-making** easier.

Technology in Operations

Marketing departments use Technology to gather Information about Customers

Many companies now use **technology** to gather **information** about the **lifestyles** of their **customers** and the **products** that they **buy** or are likely to buy. This helps them to make sure that **promotions** are **targeting** the right people and will actually cause **sales** to **increase**.

1) Lots of supermarkets offer **loyalty cards** which give customers money back according to how much they spend. One **benefit** for the supermarket is that it allows them to form a **database** of customer names and addresses which they can then use to create **mailing lists** for **direct marketing** campaigns.

2) **Loyalty cards** also tell the supermarkets what **products** a particular customer is **buying**. This means they can send out **offers** which **relate** to the kind of products that the person buys **most often**.

3) **Social networking websites** are another way that businesses can use technology to find out more about customer likes and dislikes. People who use these sites often list information about themselves, including the type of **music** they like, where they go on **holiday**, what **car** they drive etc. Companies who advertise on these sites can make their adverts visible only to the people who are **likely** to **buy** their product — this is **cheaper** and more **effective** than targeting everyone who uses the website. **Search engines** like Google™ often use targeted advertising — they show adverts that are **relevant** to the topic the user searched for.

Firms need to consider the Advantages and Disadvantages of Technology

Most companies invest a lot of money in technology. Technology is beneficial if it leads to:

1) **Increased productivity** — machines can often do tasks quicker than humans can.
2) Improved **quality**.
3) **Reduced waste** through more effective production methods.
4) More **effective** and **efficient delivery** of goods and services to the customer.
5) More **effective marketing** campaigns that target the right customers.
6) More productive **staff utilisation** — staff can be transferred to more urgent or complicated tasks.
7) **Reduced** administrative and financial **costs**.
8) **Better communications** both internally and externally.

However, introducing new technology or updating older systems can create problems:

1) **Initial costs** of technology may be **high**.
2) Technology requires **constant updating** in order to stay current, which can also be **expensive**.
3) New IT systems may create an **increased** need for **staff training**.

Practice Questions

Q1 What is meant by CAD? How can a business use it?
Q2 Give two advantages and two disadvantages of using robots.
Q3 How can social networking websites be beneficial to marketing departments?
Q4 Give two advantages and two disadvantages of using technology in business.

Exam Question

Q1 (a) Identify four areas where technology may be utilised in a company. (4 marks)

(b) Discuss how technology can be used in each of these areas to benefit the company. (12 marks)

If these pages are repetitive and boring — they're the work of a robot...

Reading through this lot is enough to make you wonder how businesses ever coped before technology came along. You need to know the two main types of technology that businesses use today, as well as the benefits and pitfalls of using technology. Robots might be cheaper than humans, but they tell lousy jokes, and are no good at making tea...

Effective Marketing

Marketing is "responsible for identifying, anticipating and satisfying consumer requirements profitably." Or so says the Chartered Institute of Marketing. **Page 78 is for AQA, OCR and WJEC. Page 79 is for AQA, Edexcel and WJEC.**

Marketing establishes Demand for a Business

1) Marketing covers **research**, **analysis**, **planning** and the **"marketing mix"**. The "marketing mix" is all the decisions a business makes about promoting and selling a product.

2) Products aren't just marketed when they first appear on the shelves. **Marketing** is a **long-term** thing — although the strategy may change, **products** are **marketed** from the **start** of their **life cycle** to the bitter **end**.

3) Most larger businesses have a specialised **marketing department** — but marketing affects all departments.

4) Marketing also covers **market research** — see p.82-83 for more on this.

Marketing is important in a Competitive Environment

1) A **competitive environment** is one where there are **lots of companies** selling **products** that are **roughly** the **same**.

2) Competition is **good** for **customers**. It forces **prices down** and tends to improve **quality** and **customer service**.

3) Firms selling goods in a competitive environment rely on **marketing** to help them get a **share** of the **market**.

4) Once they have a customer base, marketing (especially **market research**) helps them come up with **new products** and make sure that their **customers** don't **shop elsewhere**.

5) Companies invent **USPs** (**U**nique **S**elling **P**oints) for their products to persuade customers to buy their products rather than products from a competitor (there's more on USPs on p.86).

6) Companies can compete on **design** and **quality**, as well as on price. They can also use **marketing** to make sure that **customers** stay **loyal** to a particular **brand** (see p.96). These are all methods of **non-price competition**.

High Disposable Income increases the Need for Marketing

AQA only

1) **Disposable income** is the amount of money that consumers have left to spend **after** they have paid **taxes** and **pension** contributions. It tends to go up and down depending on whether the economy is strong or weak.

2) When consumers have **lots** of disposable income, they start to **buy things** they **wouldn't usually** buy — such as luxury and designer goods.

3) Manufacturers of these types of product all want to attract a **share** of this new group of customers, so they **increase** the amount that they spend on **marketing**.

4) This extra spending on marketing causes sales to rise, which leads to an **increase** in **revenue**.

5) The combination of increased revenue and a wider market means companies might consider **new forms** of **advertising** which target a bigger group of people — e.g. a national women's magazine, or billboards.

6) However, an increase in disposable income can lead to a **decrease** in demand for **cheaper**, lower quality **goods**. Manufacturers of these products might spend **more** on **marketing** to win back market share.

Globalization and Brand Awareness can affect Marketing Strategy

AQA and WJEC

1) In general, **globalization** is **good** for **large companies**, because it allows them to sell their product all over the world. **Coca-Cola®** and **McDonald's** are examples of very successful **global brands**.

2) The global market has led to **customers** being very **brand aware**. Companies often **market** major brands **differently** from the way that they market lesser-known products.

3) Successful brands, such as Nike or Cadbury, often choose to **advertise** the **brand name**, rather than a specific product. The advantage of this is that it **increases** the sales of **all** their products, not just one in particular.

4) The producers of **successful** brands tend to have a lot of **influence**. This makes it easier for them to persuade **retailers** to install special point-of-sale displays (for more on point of sale, see p.97) and gives them access to extremely high profile forms of advertising, such as **product placement** in films.

5) Some consumers **dislike** buying from large, **global companies**, because they feel that they are impersonal or too powerful. Some companies, such as HSBC, have run **marketing** campaigns which **emphasise** their ability to adapt to the **local** environment.

—— *AQA and WJEC* —————————————————— *AQA and WJEC* ——

Effective Marketing

Marketing can be aimed at Large or Small Groups of Consumers

Mass marketing is a way of trying to make sure that **as many** customers **as possible** see a particular product. **Niche marketing** tries to sell to a **smaller**, more **specific** group of people. More on niche and mass markets on p.8 and p.10.

Advantages of Niche Marketing

+   Niche marketing **only** targets people who are likely to be **interested** in the product in question. So although it only reaches a small group of consumers, there is a good chance they will want to buy the product.

+   Because it is only targeting a very limited group of customers, niche marketing is **cheaper** than mass marketing.

Disadvantages of Niche Marketing

–   Some companies selling to a niche market are forced to set a **high price** for their product. This is because their low levels of production prevent them benefiting from **economies of scale**.

–   Another disadvantage of niche marketing is that identifying a niche can be **expensive**, as well as **time-consuming**.

Advantages of Mass Marketing

+   The most obvious advantage of mass marketing is that it allows companies to reach a **huge audience**.

+   Producers of mass market products save money because of **economies of scale**. These savings can be passed on to consumers, allowing firms to **compete** on **price**.

Disadvantages of Mass Marketing

–   A mass marketing strategy is unlikely to make customers feel that a product meets their **exact needs**. **Market share** can **decrease** as niche products break the market into smaller segments.

–   Mass marketing is **expensive**, as it relies on **widespread forms** of promotion, such as TV advertising.

Companies can use Marketing to target Customers or Other Businesses

The growth of the internet has created many new types of business. Two of the most important of these are **business-to-business** (B2B) companies, and **business-to-consumer** (B2C) companies.

With a name like B2C, they would never have reached the top 40, even without the pink trumpet.

1)   B2B companies are online businesses which sell to other **businesses**. They usually sell **services**, such as help with recruitment, or **telecommunications** and **computer products**.

2)   B2C businesses, such as Amazon.com®, sell goods **directly** to the **public** via the internet.

3)   When **businesses** are **selling** to **other businesses** they try to build a good **ongoing relationship** with the customer. They want the customer to come back and make **repeat purchases**, and they may be able to make extra profit by providing **spare parts** and **servicing** as well.

4)   B2C companies use **discounts**, **advertising** and other **promotions** to persuade people to **spend money**. The aim is to get people to **buy** the product **there** and **then**.

Practice Questions

Q1   What is meant by "non-price competition"?

Q2   Give three ways in which increased brand awareness has changed the way that businesses market goods.

Q3   What kind of services and products do B2B businesses usually sell?

Exam Questions

Q1   Explain how operating globally may have an impact on a firm's marketing strategy.   (5 marks)

Q2   Justify why a business selling tie-dye T-shirts should consider a niche marketing strategy.   (4 marks)

Maybe I'll find a niche, crawl into it, and stay there forever...

You might feel like you can't get away from all this marketing stuff — companies probably feel that way too. When customers are spending more money, companies need marketing to persuade them to spend it on their products. When they spend less, marketing tries to tempt them to keep buying. If only consumers weren't such a fickle bunch...

Market Analysis and Marketing Objectives

Funny types, those marketing dudes. Always wanting to know how big it is, and how much it'll grow (market share, that is). Mind you, once they know that, they can set objectives to help increase sales. **For Edexcel, OCR and WJEC.**

Marketing helps a company to Achieve its overall Objectives

Marketing objectives are **targets** that a company's **marketing department** sets itself. They tend to **focus** on **sales**. It's not as simple as "increase sales," though — a more **realistic objective** would be something like "**make sure Product X maintains its current market share**," or "**target Product Y at a younger segment of the market**".

1) **Marketing objectives** aren't just made up. They're **based on** a combination of **market research** and **sales** and **profit forecasts** for the product in question.

2) Once you've chosen your **marketing objectives**, you need a **marketing strategy**. **Strategy** is **how** companies **achieve** their **objectives**. It's a **long-term** plan, unlike **marketing tactics**, which are the **short-term activities** that make sure the strategy is on track to succeed.

3) **Mass** and **niche marketing** are examples of **common marketing strategies**. For more on these, see p.79.

Businesses **plan marketing strategies** to achieve their objectives. They **decide** which marketing **activities** to do, based on their **research** and **analysis**.

They put their **strategies** into **action** and carry out **marketing activities**.

They **monitor sales** to make sure their marketing strategies are having the **right effect**.

They **change and improve** their marketing **strategies** and **activities** — if they **need** to.

Marketing approaches can be Product-, Market- or Asset-Oriented

1) **Product-oriented** businesses start by deciding what they can **produce**. They put the **product** ahead of **customer needs** or **budget** constraints.

2) A product-oriented approach might **save** a business **money** on **market research** but it's a **risky** strategy, because customers might want or need a **different product** altogether.

1) **Market-oriented** or **customer-oriented** businesses start by finding out what the **customer wants**.

2) A **market-oriented** approach is more likely to **succeed** than a product-oriented approach, but it requires **extensive market research**, which can be **expensive**.

1) **Asset-led marketing** considers **consumer wants** and the **strengths** (assets) of the business.

2) For example, when developing the **new Mini**, **BMW** linked the **market desire** for a new small car with their **reputation** for reliability and engineering expertise. Customers were happy to pay a **premium price**.

3) **Asset-led marketing** is now seen as the best route to long-term **customer satisfaction** and **brand loyalty**.

WJEC

WJEC

Markets are Segmented into groups of Similar Customers

Different groups of customers have different needs. Businesses **analyse** different parts (**segments**) of a market so that they can **focus** on the needs of **specific groups** within a target market. Segmentation can be done by:

1) **Income**, e.g. luxury products are aimed at high income groups.

2) **Socio-economic class**, e.g. based on the kind of jobs people have — from senior professionals to unemployed people.

3) **Age**, e.g. businesses often target products at specific age groups — teens, pre-teens, 25-35 year olds etc.

4) **Gender**, e.g. chocolate manufacturers target some items at women (e.g. Flake) and some at men (e.g. Yorkie®).

5) **Geographical region**, e.g. some goods have a regional market — you don't often see laver bread outside Wales.

6) **Amount of use**, e.g. mobile phone suppliers market differently to heavy users and light users.

7) **Ethnic grouping**, e.g. new ethnic minority TV channels make it easier to aim adverts at particular ethnic groups.

All these methods focus on a **characteristic** of the **customer**. New **segmentation** methods also categorise markets according to the **reasons** for buying a product — as an essential, to cheer yourself up, as a gift, etc. But although segmentation is useful for **identifying** potential **customers** and the best way of **marketing** a product, it can cause a firm to **ignore** the **needs** of other **potential customers**, e.g. if they target a chocolate bar at one particular gender.

Market Analysis and Marketing Objectives

Market Analysis tells a Business about the Market it's in

Market analysis lets businesses spot **opportunities** in a market by looking at **market conditions**. The most important conditions are **market size**, **growth** in the market and **market share**.

MARKET SIZE — by volume and by value

Businesses estimate the **size** of their market in terms of the **total number of sales** (volume of sales) or in terms of the **value** in pounds of **all the sales** in the market.

To calculate market size by value:

Add together the **prices** of all the sales that all the businesses in that market have made.

Market size and share have to be considered together. E.g. 10% of a £1m market is worth £100k, while 25% of a £200k market is only worth £50k.

MARKET SHARE — sales as a percentage of total market size

Businesses like to know what **share** of the market they have. If **1 out of every 4** PCs bought was a Dell™, this would mean that Dell™ had a **25% market share** (in terms of units sold). If **£1 out of every £10** spent on perfume was spent on Chanel, this would mean Chanel had a **10% market share** (in terms of sales value).

These two are measured as percentages.

To calculate market share:

$$\frac{\text{Sales}}{\text{Total market size}} \times 100\%$$

MARKET GROWTH

Businesses need to know if the market is **growing** or **shrinking**. Competition is fierce in a shrinking market — there are fewer customers to go around. In a **growing** market, **several** firms can **grow easily**. Businesses may want to get out of a market that's getting smaller.

To calculate market growth:

$$\frac{\text{New market size} - \text{old market size}}{\text{Old market size}} \times 100\%$$

As well as size, share and growth, market analysis measures things like **profitability** and the **costs** of buying equipment and training staff so you can **get into** the market (entry costs).

The more a **firm understands** about their **market**, the more likely they are to make **good marketing decisions**.

Practice Questions

Q1   What is the difference between marketing objectives and marketing strategy?

Q2   What is meant by segmenting the market?

Q3   A market sold £33m of goods last year, and £38m of goods this year. Calculate the growth in market size.

Exam Questions

Answers on p.108.

Q1   Henry Higgins is launching a new range of salmon-based ready meals. Suggest which segments of the market he should target, and explain why.   (8 marks)

Q2   Lovecocoa.co.uk sells £2 million of chocolate annually. The chocolate market is worth £19 million. Calculate Lovecocoa.co.uk's market share.   (3 marks)

The market's growing — it now sells dodgy electrical goods as well as fruit

As far as marketing is concerned, the customer is king — if you don't find out what they want, your product is unlikely to sell much at all. Which must be irritating if you've got a good idea but nobody wants to buy it. And great for the person who sent a joke memo round the office of the razor company saying six blades would be a really good idea...

Market Research

Market research is the collection and analysis of market information such as customer likes and dislikes. It's especially important before starting a new business or launching a new product — it helps prevent disastrous errors. **For all boards.**

Market Research *is done for* Three Main Reasons

1) It helps businesses **spot opportunities**. Businesses research **customer buying patterns** to help them predict what people will be buying in the future. Businesses might use **research** to help them spot growing markets to get into and declining markets to get out of. Research on customer likes and dislikes might show a gap in the market.

2) It helps them **work out what to do next**, e.g. launch a new product or advertising campaign.

3) It helps them see if their **plans are working**. A business that keeps a keen eye on customer feedback will notice if their marketing strategy is having the right effect.

> Market research can be **expensive**. **Bad market research** can lead to **disastrous business decisions**. Businesses need to **plan carefully** to make sure they get the **maximum benefit** from market research.

There's Quantitative *and* Qualitative *market research*

1) Quantitative research produces **numerical statistics** — facts and figures. It often uses multiple-choice **surveys** with questions like: "When did you last buy this product? A: in the last week, B: in the last month, C: in the last year, D: have never bought this product." Questions like these with **fixed** answers are called **closed questions**.

Closed questions with yes or no answers make analysis easier, but sometimes open questions give more informative data.

2) Qualitative research looks into the **feelings** and **motivations** of consumers. It uses **focus groups** that have in-depth discussions on a product, and asks questions like, "How does this product make you feel?" These are called **open questions**. The **answer isn't restricted** to multiple-choice options.

There's Primary *and* Secondary *market research*

Primary market research is when a business **gathers new data** (or employs someone to do it on their behalf). **Secondary market research** is done by **analysing data** that's already available.

Primary market research — find the data yourself

1) Primary data comes from **questionnaires**, **interviews**, post / phone / internet **surveys**, **focus groups** (e.g. a group of well-informed people) and by observing **consumer behaviour** (e.g. using CCTV to see how people shop).

2) **Test marketing** means launching a product in one **region** and measuring **sales** and **customer response** before launching it nationwide. Even if it's a success, firms must consider how to get people to make **repeat purchases**.

3) Companies also **analyse** the **competition** by looking at their products, prices, market share etc.

4) Primary research uses **sampling** (see p.83) to make predictions about the **whole market** based on a sample.

5) Primary data is needed to find out what consumers think of a **new product** or **advert**. You can't use secondary data because there won't be any secondary data on a brand new product.

6) Primary data is **specific** to the purpose it's needed for. This is great for **niche markets** — secondary data might be too broad or too mainstream to tell you anything useful.

7) Primary data is **exclusive** to the business who commissioned the research, so **competitors can't benefit** from it.

8) Primary research is always **up to date**.

9) **But** it is **labour-intensive**, **expensive** and **slow**.

Secondary market research — the data's already there

1) **Internal sources** of data include loyalty cards, feedback from company salesmen, analysis of company sales reports, financial accounts, and stock records.

2) **External sources** include government publications like the Social Trends report, marketing agency reports, pressure groups and trade magazines.

3) **Secondary data** is much **easier**, **faster** and **cheaper** to get hold of than primary data.

Secondary research is often called desk research.

4) **But**, secondary data that was gathered for a different purpose might be **unsuitable**. It may not be **relevant** to what the company are looking for and it may be **out of date**.

5) Secondary data is often used to get an **initial understanding** of a market. A business may then do more specific primary research to investigate any **issues** or problems that are shown up by the secondary data.

Market Research

Market researchers need a *Representative Sample*

1) Market researchers can't ask the **whole** of a **market** to fill in a survey. They select a sample.

2) When they select the sample they try to make it **represent** the market. The sample must have **similar proportions** of people in terms of things like age, income, class, ethnicity and gender. If the sample isn't representative, they've got **problems**. However, it isn't always easy to get a representative sample.

3) A **big sample** has a better **chance** of being representative than a **small sample** — but even a big sample won't be 100% representative. There's always a **margin of error**.

4) The **size** of the **sample** may depend on how many people a **company** can **afford** to ask. If the **cash** available for research is **limited**, the **risk** of the information being **inaccurate** increases.

5) **Finance** isn't the only thing which affects the **size** of the **sample** and the **sampling method**. It's also affected by the **type** of product or business, the **risk** involved and the **target market**. E.g. a company producing wedding dresses won't use random sampling (see below) as men don't form part of its target market. They're more likely to use quota sampling instead.

Random sampling is where names are selected at random.

1) **Simple Random Sample** — This is where names are picked **randomly** from a list of the whole population (or pretty close — usually from the electoral register).

Non-random sampling is... yup... when you don't pick the names at random.

1) **Quota Sample** — This is where people with certain **characteristics** are picked (say, 100 working mums between 30 and 40). Businesses use quota sampling to get opinions from the people the product is directly targeted at.

2) **Stratified Sample** — If the population contains identifiable groups with very different characteristics e.g. males and females, combining small samples from each group will give you a stratified sample.

Market research needs to *Avoid Bias*

The quality of decisions made using market research is only as good as the **accuracy** of the research.

1) Researchers have to be careful to avoid any possible **bias**.

2) Questionnaires and interviews should avoid **leading questions**. These are questions that are phrased in a way that **leads** the respondent to give a particular answer, e.g. "You do like chocolate, don't you?" Leading questions should be weeded out when designing a questionnaire.

3) Interviews suffer from "**interviewer effects**". This is when the **response** isn't what the respondent **really thinks**. This can be caused by the **personality** of the interviewer — their **opinions** can **influence** the respondent.

4) Interviewers should only ask for personal data at the **end** of an interview (unless it's needed to see if the respondent qualifies for interviewing) so that they aren't influenced by knowing anything about the respondent.

5) The more **representative** a sample is, the more **confidence** a business can have in the results of the research.

Practice Questions

Q1 Give three reasons why firms carry out market research.
Q2 What is meant by "test marketing"?
Q3 What is the difference between quantitative secondary research and qualitative primary research?
Q4 What is meant by a "leading question"?

Exam Question

Q1 Discuss why some businesses decide to pay market research companies to gather and help analyse data. (8 marks)

Surveys show that most people lie in surveys...

Research takes time and costs money — businesses must make sure the data's accurate or it'll be as much use as a chocolate fireguard. They also have to actually use the findings to provide what their customers want. If a business can use market research to increase their sales and profits, the market research will pay for itself. Everyone's a winner.

Managing a Range of Products

There's a lot to think about before bringing a new product onto the market. Businesses need the right mix of new, growing and mature products. ***This is for all four boards: AQA, WJEC, OCR and Edexcel.***

Businesses need a *Variety* of *Products* — a *Mixed Product Portfolio*

1)   A **product line** consists of related products with similar characteristics, uses or target customers.

2)   The **product mix** is the **combination** of all the **product lines** that a business produces.

3)   Businesses aim to have a **product mix** that contains a variety of different products, all at different stages of the product life cycle (p.88). That way if one product fails, the firm should still be able to depend on the others.

The *Boston Matrix* is a model of *Portfolio Analysis*

The Boston Matrix compares **market growth** with **market share**. Each **circle** in the matrix represents **one product**. The **size** of each circle represents the **sales revenue** of the product.

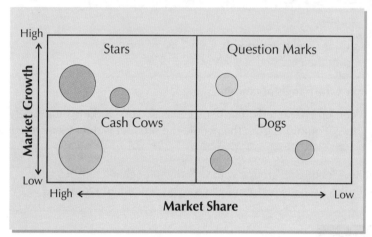

1)   All **new products** are **question marks** (sometimes called **problem children** or **wildcats**) and they have small market share and high market growth. They aren't profitable yet and could succeed or fail. They need **heavy marketing** to give them a chance. A business can do various things with question marks — **brand building**, **harvesting** (maximising sales or profit in the short term) or **divestment** (selling off the product).

2)   **Stars** have high market growth and high market share. They're in their profitable **growth** phase and have the most potential. They're future cash cows.

3)   **Cash cows** have high market share but low market growth. They're in their **maturity** phase. They've already been promoted and they're produced in high volumes, so costs are low. Cash cows bring in plenty of **money**.

Jack had low growth — so he tried standing on two legs to make himself look taller.

4)   **Dogs** have low market share and low market growth. They're usually pretty much a lost cause. If they're still profitable, e.g. a chocolate bar that is still popular, but no longer growing, the business will **harvest profit** in the **short term**. If the product is no longer making a profit it can be **sold off**.

The *Boston Matrix* is really useful

1)   The Boston Matrix lets a business see if it has a good balanced **product portfolio**. A balanced product portfolio means that a business can use money from its **cash cows** to **invest** in its **question marks** so they can become **stars**. Because the products are all related in this way, it's important to take them all into account when making decisions.

2)   The Boston Matrix **can't** always **predict exactly** what will happen to a product. A product's **cash flow** and **profit** may be **different** from what the matrix suggests (e.g. a dog may have strong cash flow and be profitable despite low or falling sales). For example, a luxury car might not sell many units and as new cars get cheaper might even lose market share, but could still make loads of money from each sale and even be selling more cars than before.

Managing a Range of Products

The Marketing Mix — Product, Price, Place, Promotion

The marketing mix describes the **factors** that firms consider when **marketing** a product. It's often known as **the 4 Ps**.

1) The marketing mix is the combination of factors that **affect** a **customer's decision** to buy. The **price** has to be right, the **product** has to be right, the product must be distributed to the right **places**, and it has to be **promoted** in the right way.

2) The factors in the marketing mix have to **work together**. Businesses may have to **compromise** on some elements — the budget for a product might not allow top-dollar spending on **all** elements of the mix.

3) A business has to be **realistic** when it's putting together its marketing mix. E.g. a business that's based in Alaska might not be able to include next-day delivery to the rest of the world in its mix.

A marketing mix with factors which work well together is called an integrated marketing mix.

The Marketing Mix is influenced by the Marketing Environment

The marketing mix needs to be **constantly reviewed** for a product to be successful or a firm to be competitive in the long term, because the environment that surrounds the marketing mix changes all the time.

1) The **marketing environment** is made up of many **different forces** which influence the marketing mix. These forces might be **legal**, **social**, **financial**, **technological** or **political**.

2) It can be hard for companies to **predict** changes in the marketing environment. Most companies **react** to changes by **adapting** their marketing mix.

3) Companies might change their marketing mix as a result of new **market research**.

4) **Political** forces include **government taxes** — the government can raise or lower tax on things like cigarettes and alcohol in its annual **budget**.

5) **Legal** forces are designed to prevent **monopolies** (see p.29) and to **protect** the consumer. They stop companies from charging excessive prices or manufacturing products that could be dangerous, e.g. clothing made of flammable fabric.

6) Advances in **technology** have two main effects. They influence the **type of products** that a company can offer and also cause **customers' aspirations** to change.

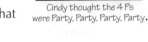
Cindy thought the 4 Ps were Party, Party, Party, Party.

7) **Financial** or economic forces affect both **consumer** and **company** spending. In times of prosperity, both consumers and businesses spend more, whereas a weak economy (high interest rates, high unemployment etc.) causes consumers to cut back and forces businesses to cut costs, too.

8) **Social** factors, like an increasing number of pensioners, or more workers from Eastern Europe affect **demand** and **consumer spending** patterns.

9) Some changes in the marketing environment are **harmful** to certain companies, but **beneficial** to others. During the 1990s, when sales of beef were affected by BSE, sales of other meats rose as customers changed their **buying habits**.

Practice Questions

Q1 What can a business do to its question marks to turn them into stars?

Q2 What is meant by "marketing mix"?

Q3 Give examples of ways in which changes in technology might influence the marketing mix.

Exam Questions

Q1 Discuss the usefulness of the Boston Matrix to a biscuit manufacturer. (10 marks)

Q2 A crisp manufacturer has just carried out marketing research which shows that consumers now want luxury crisps for dinner parties. Suggest how the firm might change its marketing mix in reaction to this. (8 marks)

Cash cows bring in plenty of money — but piggy banks do that too...

There's a lot for businesses to plan before they launch a new product — they have to be as sure as they can be that the product won't be a flop. And once it's gone from 'question mark' to 'cash cow', they need to keep an eye on the marketing environment, and adjust the marketing mix to make sure the product stays profitable.

Marketing Mix: Product

Many marketing experts think that the product is the most important element of the marketing mix. Not everyone agrees, but companies do need to develop new goods and services to keep on being successful. **For all four boards.**

New Products *can be great for a business*

There are three main reasons why it is worthwhile for companies to develop new products:

> 1) New products can bring in **new customers**.
> 2) They give a **competitive** advantage.
> 3) They allow companies to maintain a **balanced product portfolio**.

A new idea isn't necessarily a product. It can be a service, too.

Competition *and* Technology *can inspire* New Products

Most new products come about for one of three reasons:

1) **Technological developments** mean that a company can now offer the customer something that it couldn't offer before, e.g. a DVD player instead of a video player.

2) A company might develop a new product in response to a **competitor** launching something new, e.g. lots of companies developed bagless vacuum cleaners after the launch of the Dyson.

3) Somebody within the company (usually the owner or a manager) identifies a **gap in the market** (see p.82 for more on identifying gaps in the market).

There are Three *Types of* New Product

A product is considered to be 'new,' if it fits into one of the following categories:

Innovative — innovative products are completely original. Products such as **Sony's Walkman®** or 3M's Post-It® notes originally fitted into this category — when they were introduced they were **unique**.

Imitative — these are products which **copy** innovative products once they have become successful. E.g. there are lots of sticky notes and portable music players on the market now.

Replacement — a **new model** of existing product is developed and the old one is phased out. E.g. manufacturers of portable CD players are now making portable MP3 players instead.

1) In order to create **innovative products**, companies have to spend lots of money on **research and development (R&D)**.

2) They also need a **pro-active** approach to product development. This happens when a firm is attempting to be a **leader** and **create the market**. This strategy is **high risk**, but also carries the **highest potential rewards**.

Companies with innovative products often protect their ideas using patents. See p. 8.

3) The alternative approach to product development is for firms to be **reactive**. A reactive firm markets **imitative** and **replacement products**. Smaller companies usually take this approach, as they have less money to invest in R&D.

New Products *need a* Unique Selling Point (USP)

Every successful new product, whether it's innovative, imitative or a replacement for an existing product, needs to have something that **differentiates** it from the **competition**. This is known as a **Unique Selling Point** or a **Unique Selling Proposition (USP)**.

1) Products have **tangible benefits** and **intangible benefits**. Both can be used as USPs.

2) **Tangible benefits** can be **measured**. Products with tangible benefits that could be used as USPs are things like low-calorie pizza, energy-efficient fridges and savings accounts with high rates of interest.

3) **Intangible benefits** are things that can't be measured. They are based on concepts such as reputation and product image. E.g. beauty products market themselves as making the consumer feel good, certain makes of car are perceived as being reliable, and some fashion brands are seen as 'cool.'

Jim had read the whole manual, but he still couldn't find his computer's USP.

4) A product's tangible and intangible benefits are important, but there are other things the consumer considers. These might be things like **customer service**, **money-back guarantees**, and availability of **spare parts**.

5) Increasingly, companies use a product's **ethical credentials** as its USP. For example, it may have been manufactured by **fairtrade** workers or be made of **sustainable materials**. For more on ethical trading, see p.28-29.

Marketing Mix: Product

New Product Development includes Several Stages

1) **Ideas stage** — Market researchers look for a **gap in the market**, and figure out how a new product can best meet customer needs. The business does **research and development** (R&D) and analyses **competitor** products.

2) **Screening stage** — The business analyses the idea for the new product to see if it's **easy to market**, and to see if it'll make a **profit**. Market researchers find out what **consumers think** about the potential new product. A **prototype** (model) might be made to find out what the new product will look like in **real life**.

The relative importance of formal and functional design depends on the product and the market.

3) **Product development stage** — The prototype is turned into a saleable product. The **functional design** of the product (its **structure** and how it **works**) and the **formal design** (its **appearance**) are made as good as possible.

4) **Value analysis** — The business tries to make the product good **value** for money. They look at the economy of **making**, **warehousing** and **distributing** the product to make sure the whole process will be **efficient** and give value for money — for the **business** and for the **consumer**.

5) **Testing** — Just before launch, the product may be tested. A small batch of **pilot products** are made, and market research investigates **customer reactions** to them. If the public like it, the **production line** is set to make the product. Then the business **launches** the product.

Most new products Fail — it's better to fail Sooner rather than Later

New product development is **expensive**. **Limited money** often stops development. Sometimes it turns out that the product is **too expensive** to make and wouldn't be profitable.

Products that survive long enough to reach the market can create **new problems** over time:

1) **Fixed-asset** purchases often increase, because companies need new machines, factories etc. to produce the new product.

2) **Revenue expenditure** also tends to increase — the company needs to purchase materials to make the new product, and if it needs to employ extra staff, it has to pay their wages, too. This all affects the company's **liquidity** (the amount of cash it has available to use).

3) Firms can find it hard to create **customer confidence and loyalty**. Lots of customers will buy a new product once, but it can be hard to get them to make repeat purchases. This is especially true for firms which are still young.

In the first few months of their life, spending on new products is usually much higher than their revenue. This tends to even out over time.

Practice Questions

Q1 There are three types of new product. What are they called?
Q2 What is the benefit for a company of having a product with a unique selling point?
Q3 What are the stages of new product development?

Exam Questions

Q1 Explain why a small company which is new to the market might prefer to launch an imitative, rather than innovative, product. (4 marks)

Q2 Sam and Bob want to open a luxury chocolate shop, and want to make sure their product is unique. Explain what is meant by a USP and give four examples of USPs they could use for their product. (5 marks)

Most new products fail — sounds like they could do with a revision guide...

Launching a product sounds easy — if you can't come up with your own idea, you can just imitate someone else or replace something that exists already. It's tougher than it looks though, and with all those stages of product development to get through it's no wonder that most new ideas never live to see the shelves...

Marketing Mix: Product

All products are born with no sales at all. If they're looked after, they grow into big strong products with lots of sales, then they get married and have lots of spin-offs ... er, maybe. **For all four boards: AQA, WJEC, OCR and Edexcel.**

Products *have a* Life Cycle

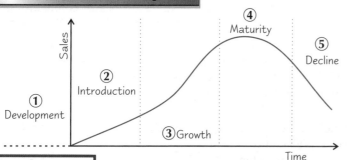

The product life cycle shows the **sales** of a product over **time**. It's useful for planning **marketing strategies** and changing the **marketing mix**.

1 — Development

1) The **research and development** (R&D) department **develop** the product.
2) The **marketing** department does **market research**.
3) The **costs** are **high**, and there aren't any sales yet to cover the costs.
4) Development has a **high failure rate**. This is because there's often **not enough demand**, or because the business can't make the product **cheaply** enough to make a profit.

2 — Introduction

1) The product is **launched**, either in one market or in several markets. It's sometimes launched with **complementary** products — e.g. the PlayStation® was launched with games.
2) The business often **promotes** the product heavily to build sales — but businesses need to make sure they've got enough **resources** and **capacity** to **meet the demand** that promotions create.
3) The **initial price** of the product may be **high** to cover **promotional costs**. This is called **skimming the market**.
4) Alternatively, the price can start off **low** to encourage sales. This is **penetration pricing**.
5) Sales go up, but the sales revenue has to pay for the high **fixed cost** of development **before** the product can make a **profit**. The business usually ditches products with disappointing sales after this stage.
6) There aren't many **outlets** for the new product.
7) Competition may be **limited** (if it's an **innovative** product).

3 — Growth

1) Sales grow fast. There are **new customers** and **repeat** customers.
2) **Economies of scale** mean the price of manufacturing a unit goes down the more you make, so **profits rise**.
3) The **pricing** strategy may change to a longer-term **cost-based** pricing method (see p.90).
4) **Competitors** may be attracted to the market. Promotion shows **differences** from the competitors' products.
5) The product is often **improved** or **developed**.
6) Rising sales encourage **more outlets** to stock the product.

4 — Maturity

1) **Sales** reach a **peak** and profitability increases because **fixed costs** of **development** have been **paid for**.
2) At **saturation** (when the market is full and has reached maximum growth) sales may begin to drop, depending on the product. Sales are more likely to drop for long-lasting products that customers do not need to replace regularly. The price is often reduced to stimulate **demand**, which reduces profits.
3) There aren't many new customers. **Competition** within the industry becomes fierce — again sales might **suffer**.

5 — Decline

1) The product doesn't **appeal** to customers any more. **Sales fall** rapidly and profits decrease.
2) On the other hand, the product may just stay profitable if **promotional costs** are **low** enough.
3) If sales carry on falling, the product is **withdrawn** or **sold** to another business (selling a product to another company is called **divestment**).

Marketing Mix: Product

Extension Strategies keep a product Going Strong for Longer

Extension strategies try to prolong the life of the product by changing the **marketing mix**. They include:

1) **Product development** — businesses **improve**, reformulate or **redesign** a product. They can change the design of **packaging** to make it look more up to date, or make **special editions** of the product. This can also give a **new focus** to existing **marketing** campaigns.

2) **Market development** — businesses can find **new markets** or **new uses** for existing products, for example by aiming a product at a new market **segment** (e.g. selling baby oil and baby powder for adult use).

3) A business can change the way the product's **distributed** — by selling through the **internet**, selling through **supermarkets** or convenience stores, etc.

4) A business can change the way the product's **priced**.

5) A business can change the way they **promote** the product — by running a new **ad campaign**, for example.

> **Decline isn't inevitable** — it's usually caused by products becoming obsolete, changing consumer tastes or poor marketing. Quality products with excellent original design (e.g. Cadbury's Dairy Milk) can continue selling for **decades**.

Cash Flow Depends on the Product Life Cycle stage

Cash flow is the difference between **money coming in** and **money going out**. Money comes in from **outside investment** (especially at the start of the life cycle) and from **sales** (mostly later on). Money goes out as **fixed** and **variable costs**. If more money comes in than goes out, cash flow is **positive**. If more goes out than comes in, cash flow is **negative**.

1) At the **development** stage, cash flow is likely to be **negative**. Money is being spent on research and development and there aren't any sales to cover costs.

2) At **introduction**, cash flow is still **negative**. The product is likely to have **cost more** than it makes in sales.

3) As the product goes into the **growth** phase, **cash flow perks up**. Promotion costs should go down, and at the same time sales should be increasing.

4) When the product is in the **maturity** phase, cash flow is **positive**. Sales are **high** and unit **costs** are **low**.

5) In the **decline** phase, sales fall and this might lead to cash flow becoming **negative** again.

Not all products follow the Same Cycle ——— WJEC ———

1) The **graph** on the opposite page is **just one example** of what a product life cycle might look like. The **shape** of the **curve** can **change** a lot, because some products, like the cigarette, are in the maturity phase for years and years, while others, like the Tamagotchi, go into decline in just a few months.

2) Because the product life cycle can vary so dramatically, it's **not** much **good** for **forecasting sales**.

3) Another **disadvantage** is that the cycle can be **self-fulfilling**. If a product's sales seem to be declining, managers might cut its advertising budget, causing it to decline even faster.

——— WJEC ——————————————————— WJEC ———

Practice Questions

Q1 What are the stages of the product life cycle?

Q2 What are extension strategies?

Q3 What happens to cash flow during the growth stage of a product's life cycle?

Q4 Why does profitability increase in the maturity phase of the product life cycle?

Exam Questions

Q1	Describe what happens to cash flow during a product's life cycle.	(5 marks)
Q2	To what extent are declining sales inevitable for products?	(10 marks)

If a product can't ride a bike, does it still have a cycle...

There's a lot to learn on these pages, I'll give you that. If you take it step by step, it's fairly straightforward — it just goes through the product life cycle and says what's going on at each stage. And if you know the product life cycle inside out, it won't be so hard to learn about the problems with it, or how it affects cash flow. Or that's the theory.

Marketing Mix: Price

The basic rules of pricing are obvious — a firm needs to price its product so that it covers its costs but is still affordable for the consumer. Products often change price at different stages in their life cycle. **For AQA, OCR and WJEC.**

Cost-plus and Contribution Pricing are Cost-based Pricing Methods

These pricing strategies both determine **prices** according to a company's **production costs**.

1) **Cost-plus pricing** involves adding the direct and indirect costs of production together and then adding a **fixed percentage** called a **mark-up**.

2) **Contribution pricing** sets the price to be more than the **variable costs** per unit. The price of each unit makes a **contribution** towards the **overheads** (fixed costs) of the business.

Cost-based pricing adds a bit onto the cost of production to come up with a selling price.

The main **benefit** of using cost-based methods of pricing is that companies can be sure of **covering** their **production costs**. The **disadvantage** is that they fail to take into account **outside influences** — if a **competitor's price** is more appealing, the consumer may well choose to buy the competitor's product instead.

— **OCR only** —

Price Discrimination means charging Different Customers Different Prices

When a company sells its product at different prices to different groups of consumers, this is called **price discrimination**.

1) Price discrimination often occurs when consumers are **buying a service in advance**. Hotel rooms, air travel and rail tickets are all examples of this. Prices change as the **departure date gets nearer**. They can also change according to the **day** or **time** that a customer wants to travel.

2) Other companies might vary prices according to the **age** or **social status** of their customers. **Theatres**, **cinemas** and **theme parks** sell tickets at different rates to **OAPs**, **students**, **under-16s** and **families**.

3) The advantage of price discrimination is that it allows companies to **respond quickly to changes in demand**. If demand is high at a particular time, prices rise, and if demand is low, prices go down. It also allows firms to offset some of the costs of having **excess capacity**.

4) Companies need to make sure it is possible to **separate out the different markets** before using price discrimination. Building merchants, e.g. Ridgeons, sell to businesses at lower prices, so they need to be able to tell the difference between their trade and private customers. Otherwise they might sell to private customers at trade prices by mistake.

Cheap theatre tickets — one reason why it's great to be old.

Existing Products can be either Price Leaders or Takers

Strategies for existing products:

1) A **price leader** is an existing brand that's in such a **powerful position** within the market that it sets the price, and other businesses follow. Rival businesses know that consumers see the price leader as **the** brand of tea bags or baked beans, so they'll have to price their own rival product a tiny bit lower or nobody will buy it.

2) **Competition** reduces prices. In very competitive markets, **buyers dictate the price**, and sellers have to **take whatever price** the buyer is willing to pay — this is called **price taking**. E.g. milk producers selling to supermarkets are **price takers**.

3) **Predatory pricing** is when a business **deliberately lowers prices** to force another business **out of the market** — e.g. a large nationwide company might target a successful but small local competitor by lowering their prices in that area until the small competitor **goes out of business**. Prices can stay high in all other areas, so the business will lose little money overall, and once the competitor has gone they will **raise** their prices again.

4) **Competitive pricing** is when companies **monitor** their **competitors' prices** to make sure that their own prices are set at an equal or lower level. **Supermarkets** and **department stores** often use this method. Some stores will **refund the difference** in price if you are able to find a product cheaper somewhere else.

Marketing Mix: Price

Psychological Pricing and Loss Leaders help to attract More Customers

Businesses use certain **tactics** to ensure they make profitable sales. For example:

1) **Psychological pricing** bases the price on customers' **expectations** about what to pay. For example, a high price may make people think the product is high quality, and £99.99 seems better than £100 even though it's only 1p difference.

2) **Loss leaders** are products sold at or below cost price. These products may well **lose money**, but the idea is that they'll make a profit for the business indirectly, e.g. by enticing customers into the shop where they'll probably buy full-priced items too. The loss leaders can be widely advertised to encourage this. This tactic can work well in **supermarkets**, where customers will usually buy lots of other items as well as the loss leader.

Companies use Promotional Pricing Strategies when launching New Products

1) **New and innovative products** are often sold at **high prices** when they first reach the market. This is known as **skimming**, or **creaming**. Consumers will pay more because the product has **scarcity value**, and the high price boosts the **product's image** and increases its appeal. New **technological products**, such as computers, tend to be priced using this method. Prices are then dropped quite considerably when the product has been on the market for a year or so, but economies of scale (see p.60-61) can help make up for the drop in revenue.

2) **Skimming** is a good strategy to use if a company can **protect its product** to make sure competitors don't launch an imitative product at a lower price. They might use **patents** or **trademarks** to stop other people copying their idea.

3) **Penetration pricing** is the opposite of skimming. It means launching a product at a **low price** in order to **attract customers** and gain **market share**. It is especially effective in markets which are **price sensitive**.

4) **Penetration pricing** works best for companies that can benefit from **economies of scale** (see p.60-61) when manufacturing large quantities of a product.

Several Factors affect Demand for a Product

1) The **price of the product** affects demand. As the price goes up, demand tends to go down. As the price goes down, demand goes up.

2) The **price of similar products** affects demand. When one manufacturer increases its prices, demand for **cheaper competitor products** tends to **rise**.

3) **Customer income** affects demand. When people have **more money to spend**, there's more demand.

4) **Seasonality** affects demand. E.g. the demand for soft drinks is greater in the **summer**.

5) Successful **marketing** stimulates demand.

Maria had a problem with customer income — no customers ever came in.

Practice Questions

Q1 Give one advantage and one disadvantage of using a cost-based pricing method.

Q2 What is the difference between a price leader and a price taker?

Q3 What kind of products tend to be sold using the skimming method?

Q4 Give three examples of factors other than price which affect demand.

Exam Questions

Q1 A hotel is pricing its rooms according to the cost-plus method. Explain why it might benefit from switching to price discrimination.

(6 marks)

Q2 A small company is launching a new brand of fruit juice. Suggest which pricing methods it should consider, and explain why.

(6 marks)

Skimming and creaming — both ways of milking profits...

When it comes to pricing, most companies use a cost-based method and throw in the occasional bit of promotional pricing to keep consumers interested. The key point to remember is that price isn't the only thing that bothers customers — a lot of people would rather buy high quality chicken nuggets than cheap ones made of scrawny bits of chicken neck.

Marketing Mix: Price

OK, so price isn't the only thing that affects demand, but it can certainly have a pretty major impact. Just how big or small that impact is depends on the price elasticity of demand. ***For all four boards.***

Price Elasticity of Demand shows how Demand changes with Price

1) **Price elastic** products have a **large percentage change in demand** for a **small percentage change in price**.

2) **Price inelastic** products are the opposite — there's a **small percentage change in demand** for a **big percentage change in price**.

$$\text{Price elasticity of demand} = \frac{\text{\% change in quantity demanded}}{\text{\% change in price}}$$

If you're doing the AQA exam, they won't ask you to do this calculation. They'll give you the elasticity coefficient and you just need to use it to say how price change affects revenue.

Example: A price **rise** of **10%** results in a **30% reduction** in demand.

$$\text{Price elasticity of demand} = \frac{-30\%}{+10\%} = -3$$

Price **elastic**, because the price elasticity of demand is **more than 1** (ignoring the minus sign).

Basically, as price goes up demand falls, and vice versa.

Example: A price **reduction** of **20%** results in a **5% increase** in demand.

$$\text{Price elasticity of demand} = \frac{+5\%}{-20\%} = -0.25$$

Price **inelastic**, because the price elasticity of demand is **less than 1**.

This is called the elasticity coefficient

3) Price elasticity of demand is **always negative**, so ignore the minus sign. A positive change in price causes a negative change in demand, and a negative change in price causes a positive change in demand.

4) If the price elasticity of demand is **greater than 1** (ignoring the minus sign), the product is **price elastic**. If the price elasticity of demand is **less than 1**, it's **price inelastic**. So, −3 is price elastic and −0.25 is price inelastic.

Price Elasticity affects Revenue and Profit

1) **Sales revenue = price** of product × **quantity sold**. Price elasticity shows how price affects sales revenue.

2) If demand is **price elastic**, a **price increase** will make **sales revenue go down**.
The **% decrease in sales** will be **more** than the **% increase in price**.

3) If demand is price **inelastic**, a rise in **price** will make **sales revenue go up**.
The % decrease in sales isn't big enough to offset the % increase in price.

4) If demand is **price elastic**, a firm can **increase revenue** by reducing price, which then greatly increases the number of sales. **But profit = revenue − cost**, and more sales often mean **higher costs**. The **profits** will only increase if the **rise in revenue** is **more** than the **rise** in **costs**.

5) If demand is **price inelastic**, increasing the price will make **sales go down slightly**, but **sales revenue go up**. Because there are **fewer sales**, there are **lower costs**. This means that there's **more profit**.

Price change	PED more than 1 (elastic)	PED equal to 1	PED less than 1 (inelastic)
Increase in price	Sales revenue decreases	Sales revenue doesn't change	Sales revenue increases
Decrease in price	Sales revenue increases	Sales revenue doesn't change	Sales revenue decreases

This table shows how price changes affect sales revenue.

Example: A company makes scarves and sells them for £11. Annual sales are 9600 scarves. The product's elasticity coefficient is −2.5. If they increase the price to £12.10, calculate the change in revenue.

Current revenue: £11 × 9600 = £105 600

% change in quantity demanded: 10% change in price x 2.5 elasticity coefficient = 25% decrease

25% of 9600: 9600 x 0.25 = 2400 **New sales:** 9600 − 2400 = 7200 **New revenue** = 7200 x £12.10 = £87 120

Change in revenue: £105 600 − £87 120 = £18 480 decrease in revenue

It can be Hard to Work Out price elasticity of demand

1) Estimating price elasticity of demand is **difficult** because price isn't the **only** factor affecting demand. An increase in demand for ice cream could be partly down to **hot weather** and a good **advertising** campaign.

2) Businesses use **primary market research** (see p.82) to ask people if they'd buy a product for a **higher** or **lower price**. This gives an idea of the relationship between **price** and **demand**. **However**, surveys can be **unreliable** (people generally say they'd like things a bit cheaper than they would actually be willing to pay).

3) The values used in price elasticity calculations may be wrong. The calculations are often based on **estimates** of percentage change in price and demand, or on **unrepresentative** data — the market may have **changed** since the data was collected.

Marketing Mix: Price

Price elasticity of demand Depends on Ease of Switching Brands

1) If a consumer can **easily switch** to a **competitor** product, the demand will be **price elastic** when there is a **rise in price**. Customers will buy the **competitor's product** instead.

2) Businesses try to **differentiate** their products to create **brand loyalty**. **Loyal** customers won't switch even if the price goes up, so this makes the demand **less** price elastic.

3) It's easier for customers to switch if they can **compare prices** and find cheaper alternatives. The **internet** makes it easier to switch and **increases price elasticity**.

4) People tend not to switch to alternatives in the **short term**. They **take time** to get **fed up** with a product.

5) **Product types** tend to be **price inelastic**, but individual **brands** tend to be **price elastic**. For example, **petrol** sales are **inelastic** because all cars need fuel. The sales of an **individual company's petrol** are **elastic** because motorists can easily go to a **cheaper filling station**.

Income Elasticity of Demand shows how Demand changes with Income

When people earn **more money**, there's **more demand** for some products.
Funnily enough, there's **less demand** for other products.

You'll need to know this equation whichever exam board you're doing.

$$\text{Income elasticity of demand} = \frac{\%\ \text{change in quantity demanded}}{\%\ \text{change in real incomes}}$$

Change in real income means change in income, taking into account how prices have changed (usually increased) over the same period (this is inflation — see p.26).

Example: A rise in income of **10%** results in a **5% increase** in demand.

$$\text{Income elasticity of demand} = \frac{+5\%}{+10\%} = +0.5$$

1) **Normal goods** have a **positive income elasticity of demand** that's **less than 1**. This means that as **income rises**, the **demand** for normal goods **rises** — but at a **slower rate** than the increase in income.

2) **Luxury goods** have a **positive income elasticity of demand** which is **more than 1**. This means that the **demand for luxury goods** grows **faster** than the increase in income.

3) In a business sense, "**inferior**" goods are cheaper, 'value' products — taking a **coach** instead of the **train**, for example or eating a **cheaper supermarket value brand** of baked beans because you can't afford **Heinz baked beans**. Inferior goods have a **negative income elasticity of demand** — **demand falls** when **income rises** and **demand rises** when **income falls**.

Elasticity helps a business make Choices

1) **Price elasticity** helps a manufacturer **decide** whether to **raise** or **lower** the price of a product. They can see what might happen to the sales, and ultimately what will happen to sales revenue.

2) **Income elasticity** helps a manufacturer see what'll happen to sales if the **economy** grows or shrinks.

Practice Questions

Q1 If a product has an elasticity coefficient of –0.9, is it elastic or inelastic?

Q2 Give two reasons why it can be difficult to calculate price elasticity.

Q3 What kind of products become less popular when there's an increase in income?

Answer on p.108.

Exam Questions

Q1 A company sells 200 horses a year for £1500 each. If the elasticity coefficient is –0.7, calculate the impact on revenue that a 15% increase in prices will have.
(9 marks)

Q2 Explain why product differentiation reduces elasticity of demand.
(3 marks)

Rubber prices are usually the most elastic...

The clues are in the names with these two — price elasticity shows how much price influences demand, and income elasticity shows how much demand is affected by income. The method for working out changes in revenue using the elasticity coefficient has quite a few steps, so make sure you get your head round that one...

Marketing Mix: Place

Distribution is important. This is the "place" part of the marketing mix. If a product can't get to the marketplace, no one can buy it. Needs go unfulfilled, companies don't make profits, anarchy reigns... **For all four boards.**

You have to get the **Product** to the **Consumer**

A **channel** of **distribution** is the route a product takes from the producer to the consumer. A product usually passes through **intermediaries** on the way from producer to consumer — e.g. **retailers**, **wholesalers** and **agents**.

1) **Retailers** are **shops** who sell to consumers. They're usually the **final stage** in the distribution channel. Tesco, Argos and Amazon.co.uk® are **retailers**. Retailers can be physical shops or online "e-tailers".

2) **Wholesalers** buy products cheaply in **bulk** and **sell them on** to **retailers**.
Wholesalers make life **easier** for retailers and manufacturers:

- Wholesalers **buy** goods from manufacturers in bulk and **sell** them in **smaller quantities** to **retailers**. This is called **"breaking bulk"** — a wholesaler takes the goods off the manufacturer's hands and **pays** for the whole lot. Manufacturers don't have to **wait** for customers to buy the goods before they see any cash.

- Wholesalers make distribution **simpler**. Without a wholesaler, the manufacturer would have to make **separate deliveries** to lots of retailers, and send every retailer an **invoice**. Selling to one wholesaler cuts down the paperwork and the number of journeys.

- Wholesalers can **store more goods** than a retailer can — they act as the retailer's storage cupboard.

3) **Agents** act on behalf of **manufacturers**. See below for more about the role of an agent.

There are **Different Channels of Distribution**

Channels of distribution have different levels. It's more expensive, but sometimes necessary, to have a **multi-layered** channel.

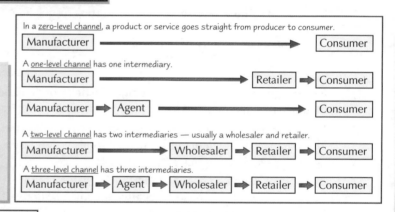

In a zero-level channel, a product or service goes straight from producer to consumer.
Manufacturer → Consumer

A one-level channel has one intermediary.
Manufacturer → Retailer → Consumer
Manufacturer → Agent → Consumer

A two-level channel has two intermediaries — usually a wholesaler and retailer.
Manufacturer → Wholesaler → Retailer → Consumer

A three-level channel has three intermediaries.
Manufacturer → Agent → Wholesaler → Retailer → Consumer

Direct Selling: Manufacturer → Consumer

Accountants, electricians and hairdressers sell their **services** direct to the consumer. The **internet** has made it **easier** for producers of goods to sell **direct** to the consumer. Direct selling is now very popular, and is also done through door-to-door sales, TV shopping channels, telephone sales and mail-order catalogues.

Indirect Selling: Manufacturer → Retailer → Consumer

Large supermarkets buy goods in bulk direct from the manufacturer and have them delivered either straight from the manufacturer or via their own warehouses.

Indirect Selling: Manufacturer → Wholesaler → Retailer → Consumer

This is the **traditional** distribution channel used for **fast moving consumer goods** (known as FMCG for short).

Direct Selling through an agent: Manufacturer → Agent → Consumer

An agent is like a sales representative, except they are not employed by the company whose goods they sell. They get commission (a percentage of the value of the goods they sell) instead of being paid a salary. Ann Summers lingerie is sold by **agents** through **party plans** — people invite friends to their **home** and an **agent** sells the goods **at the party**. Some **mail-order catalogues** (e.g. Avon) use agents who place orders on behalf of other people and collect payments from them.

Retailers often use **Several Channels of Distribution**

Many firms now sell goods via the internet. Having an online store can affect the way a company distributes goods.

1) Stores which **only** sell **online** may have **cheaper costs**, because they use a **single** channel of distribution. However they can have **problems** establishing **brand loyalty**.

2) Companies such as supermarkets and fashion retailers which have high street stores as well as an internet store are using a **multi-channel strategy**. This may lead to added costs if they are supplying goods from different warehouses, but it also allows them to target a wider market.

3) For small businesses, a low-cost option is to sell goods using **auction sites** or **e-marketplaces** (e.g. eBay™).

Marketing Mix: Place

Businesses choose a *Channel* of *Distribution* to *Suit Their Needs*

The choice of distribution channel is a compromise between cost, ease and control.

1) It's **more profitable** to **sell direct** to the customer. Each **intermediary** (party) in the distribution chain takes a **slice of profit** from the manufacturer — wholesalers and retailers have to make money too. Businesses that **sell direct** can offer their product at a **lower price** than **retailers** at the end of a long distribution chain.

2) On the other hand, it's **easier** to use **intermediaries**. It'd be a hassle to distribute a small amount of product to lots of little shops. It's easier to sell to a **wholesaler** who can deliver products from several manufacturers in a single delivery. Using a wholesaler gives a manufacturer the chance of more **market coverage**.

3) The **fewer intermediaries** in the distribution chain, the more **control** a manufacturer has over how its products are sold. It has more say in the **final selling price** and how the product is **promoted**.

4) UK **retail trends** have **changed** in recent years, as retailers have found **cheaper** or **more effective** ways of distributing their products. **Out-of-town retail parks**, **concessions** (shops within shops), and **mail-order catalogues** have **cheaper overheads** than high street stores and can sometimes offer customers other **benefits**, such as **free parking**. **Factory outlets** allow firms to make a return on **imperfect goods** (seconds) or **last season's stock**.

There are no real hard and fast rules about which distribution channel a business might choose, but there are a few trends.

Short Distribution Channels	Long Distribution Channels
Industrial products	Consumer products
Few customers	Many customers
Customers concentrated in one place	Customers widely spread out
Expensive, complex goods	Inexpensive, simple goods
Infrequent sales	Frequent sales
Bulky products	Small products
Bespoke (made to measure) products	Standard products
Services	Goods

Businesses set **distribution targets**. They might set a target of £X worth of sales through supermarkets, or selling to more retail outlets in a particular area of the country.

Businesses can use a number of **different strategies** to **achieve** their distribution targets, e.g. offering discounts to particular retailers, or using advertising in trade magazines.

Different Distribution Strategies *suit different products*

1) **Everyday groceries** and **convenience** items need to be distributed as **widely** as possible. Consumers want to be able to buy things like a newspaper, a pint of milk and a bar of chocolate at a convenient local shop. They don't want to travel 20 miles to a "Pints Of Milk R Us" superstore.

2) **Luxury** goods don't need to be widely distributed. Manufacturers of luxury goods like to sell them in a small number of **exclusive** shops — it's about **quality**, not quantity.

3) Specialist goods like electrical products need to be distributed to **specialist** shops. Consumers like to be able to **compare** several different kinds of computer or CD player before buying, and often need specialist advice and assistance when choosing what to buy.

Practice Questions

Q1 What is the role of a wholesaler?

Q2 Name two types of distribution channel.

Q3 What kind of distribution channel is traditionally used for FMCG?

Q4 What kind of distribution strategy is needed for everyday groceries?

Exam Questions

Q1 Analyse the different factors a firm must consider when deciding on an appropriate channel of distribution. (8 marks)

Q2 Evaluate internet sales as a distribution channel for luxury consumer goods. (7 marks)

I'm a new product — get me out of here...

Distribution can seem like a mundane, boring thing. Yes, it is all about warehouses full of cardboard boxes, fleets of trucks going from A to B and little men popping catalogues through your letterbox. But on the other hand it's a vital part of the wondrous marketing mix. Where you can buy something is a big factor in deciding whether to buy it, for most people.

Marketing Mix: Promotion

Promotion — using advertising, branding, sales promotion and PR to sell more products. **For all boards.**

Promotion is part of the Marketing Mix

1) Promotion is designed either to **inform** customers about a product or service, or to **persuade** them to buy it.

2) **Promotional objectives** include increasing **sales** and **profits**, or increasing **awareness** of the product.

3) All promotion has to get the customer's **attention** so that they can be informed or persuaded about the product.

Above-the-Line Promotion is Advertising through the Media

1) Advertising is **non-personal communication** from a business to the public.

2) Adverts are used to **promote goods and services** — and also to promote a firm's **public image**.

3) Advertising uses **media** such as print, TV, radio, billboards and the internet.

4) The choice of media depends partly on the **number of target customers** and the number of **readers** or **viewers** who'll **see** the advert. Ideally, a business wants its adverts to be seen by as **much** of the target market as possible.

5) The **impact** of an advert is very important. The impact of a TV ad varies depending on what time it's shown, and an advert that covers a two-page spread in a magazine has much more impact than a small ad in the classified section at the back.

6) Advertising **costs** a business **money**. The cost of an advertising campaign must be **worth it** in terms of the **extra sales** it creates. TV adverts at prime viewing times are very expensive. Ads shown when fewer people are watching are cheaper, but don't reach as many people.

7) **Specialist media** are used to advertise specialist products to **niche markets**. For example, a manufacturer of fish hooks should advertise in a fishing magazine, not the Daily Telegraph newspaper.

8) **Mass media** are mainly used to advertise **mass market consumer** products and services. However, **business** equipment like office stationery is also advertised on **TV** these days.

9) There are **legal constraints** on advertising some products. E.g. firms are not allowed to suggest that alcohol can make people socially or sexually successful. Cigarette advertising is banned altogether.

10) The **Advertising Standards Agency (ASA)** regulates advertising. It makes sure that adverts **do not mislead**, do not cause **offence**, are **socially responsible** and have regard for **fair competition**.

Advertising changes during a Product Life Cycle

See p.88-89 for more on product life cycles.

1) Products are often heavily advertised at **launch**. If a product is completely **new** to the market, the adverts are **informative**. They tell customers about the product.

2) During the **growth** phase, advertising **differentiates** between brands. It persuades consumers that the product is different from and better than competitor products. The objective of advertising in the growth phase is to **maintain** or **increase market share**.

3) When a product is at the **mature**, **saturation** phase, consumers need to be **reminded** of it. If the manufacturer has an **extension** strategy, they advertise to tell consumers about **improvements** they've made to the product.

Packaging is a crucial element of the Marketing Mix

1) **Packaging** is often referred to as the "**fifth P**," because it can be extremely useful when marketing a product.

2) **Packaging** can **give information** about a product's **tangible** and **intangible** benefits (see p.86 for more about these). It tells the consumer a lot about the product's **image**, but gives information about **what it does**, too.

3) Recently, **social trends** have forced more businesses to consider the **impact** they are having on the **environment**. Companies may try to **reduce** their packaging, or make sure it can be **recycled**.

Branding is a key aspect of Product Image

Branding can be very useful — not only does it give a product an identity, but it differentiates it from the competition.

1) **Homogenous (generic)** products are the same no matter which business sells them. Brands are **unique**.

2) Brands are important because customers pay a **premium price** for them, and customers are **loyal** to them. Brands have a specific **brand image** — a good brand has a lot of **intangible benefits** for the customer.

3) Brands can be **individual** products — like Sprite® or KitKat. "Family brands" like Heinz include a **range** of products.

Marketing Mix: Promotion

Below-the-Line promotion is advertising which Doesn't use the Media

1) Manufacturers often offer **sales promotions**. These are things like **special offers**, e.g. "buy one get one free" (**BOGOF**), competitions, free gifts, **sponsorship**, and **trade-ins**. Sales promotions can be aimed straight at the **customer** to **raise awareness** or **increase sales** of a product. Manufacturers also aim sales promotions at the **retailer** to encourage them to **stock** more of their products.

2) **Merchandising** means ensuring that retailers are displaying a company's products as effectively as possible. Some merchandisers offer retailers **point of sale displays** (e.g. special colourful racks with the company logo).

3) **Direct mail** means **mailshots** sent out to customers. The customer usually hasn't **asked** to receive them. Businesses that keep information about their customers on a database can **target** their direct mail to particular consumer groups. Direct mail that is untargeted ("**junk mail**") can sometimes be a **waste of money**, because it often just gets thrown away.

4) **Personal selling** or **direct selling** is personal communication between a **salesperson** and a customer. Personal selling includes sales assistants in shops as well as travelling salespeople and phone salespeople.

5) **Event sponsorship** makes consumers aware of a firm and its product. It also gives the firm a good image.

6) **Direct Response TV Marketing** encourages consumers to contact the advertiser directly to purchase a product they have seen advertised on television. **Shopping channels** are an example of this kind of promotion.

PR gets Businesses or Products Good Publicity in the Media

Public relations (PR) is a key form of below-the-line promotion. Many companies have **specialist PR departments**.
1) PR involves **liaising** with the **media**, writing **press releases** and answering **enquiries** from the press.
2) PR departments write **brochures**, **newsletters** and **leaflets** giving information about the company.
3) Public relations deals with events such as **product launches**, **conferences** and other **special events**.

The Promotional Mix reflects Product, Budget and Competitor Activity

1) Businesses use a **mixture** of methods to promote products. The combination of promotional techniques that a business uses to promote a product is called the **promotional mix**. The main elements in the mix are often **personal selling** and **advertising**. Other methods have a supporting role.

2) The promotional mix depends on: the **product** itself, the **market**, **competitor activity**, the **product life cycle** (see p.88-89) and the **budget** available.

3) In general, **inexpensive**, **simple** products purchased by the **consumer** are promoted by **advertising**.

4) **Expensive** and **complex** products are more likely to be promoted by **personal selling**. So are products or services sold in the **industrial market**.

5) **Consumer durables**, for example **cars** or **washing machines**, are often sold using a combination of **advertising** and **personal selling**. TV, print and billboard adverts **attract the buyer** into the showroom, where the salesperson moves in for the sale. This is called **through-the-line** promotion.

6) Manufacturers use different methods to sell their product to a **retailer**, than to sell it to the **final customer**. Businesses often use **salespeople** to get **shops** to stock their product, and **advertising** to persuade **customers** to buy the product in the shops.

Practice Questions

Q1 What two things is promotion designed to do?
Q2 In which phase of the product life cycle does advertising stress differences with competitor products?
Q3 What is meant by "PR"?

Exam Questions

Q1 Discuss how a business might change its advertising according to a product's position in its life cycle. (4 marks)

Q2 Analyse how a manufacturer of breakfast cereal could promote its product, if it did not want to advertise. (10 marks)

We want people to buy our product — that's why we tell them to BOGOF...

When it comes to promotion, it's all in the mix. You'll need to suggest which combination of methods would best suit a firm, and why. It's important to consider budget too — most companies can't afford to have David Beckham in their ads.

Understanding Statistics

There are loads of statistics involved in running a business, so you need to be able to understand what they mean.
These pages are for AQA, OCR, Edexcel and WJEC.

Businesses produce lots of Statistics

1) Businesses have a lot of **figures** — e.g. figures for sales, costs, revenues and profit, and market research data.

2) Businesses often deal with **large numbers** — e.g. profits for a small business could be thousands or tens of thousands of pounds (thousand can be written as "k", so £15k means 15 thousand pounds). Big businesses might have very large numbers for sales or revenue figures — millions (a thousand thousand, or 1 000 000) or even billions (a thousand million, or 1 000 000 000).

Remember that negative numbers are written in brackets in cash flow forecasts and variance tables.

3) Businesses need to understand what their figures **mean** so that they know how well the business is **performing**, and can forecast how well it will perform in the **future**. In order to understand the data and be able to use it, they present it in a way that makes it **easy** to understand.

Diagrams make data Easier to Understand

1) **Pie charts** are used for showing **market share**. Each **1% share** is represented by a **3.6°** section of the pie (because there's 360° in a circle and 360 ÷ 100 = 3.6). Pie charts are **simple to use** and **easy** to **understand**. They can be created quickly using **spreadsheets**.

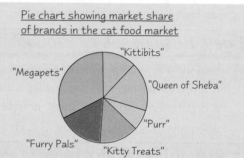

Pie chart showing market share of brands in the cat food market

"Kittibits" "Megapets" "Queen of Sheba" "Purr" "Furry Pals" "Kitty Treats"

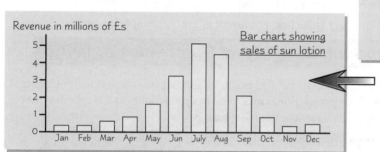

Revenue in millions of £s

Bar chart showing sales of sun lotion

2) **Bar charts** show different values for a **single variable**. They're **easy** to **construct**, easy to **interpret** and they have **high visual impact**.

3) A **histogram** looks quite similar to a bar chart. However, in a histogram the **area** of each block is proportional to the value of the variable measured (not just the height), and there are no gaps between the blocks. So a histogram is different from a bar chart because the bars can vary in both **width** and **height**. Histograms are suitable for comparing variables with **large ranges**.

4) A **pictogram** is a bar chart or histogram where the bars are **pictures** — logos or images. Pictograms are often used in **corporate brochures** — e.g. Cadbury might use pictures of their choccie bars in their sales charts.

5) **Line graphs** plot one variable against another — e.g. sales against time. **More lines** can be added on to show **more variables** — they should be in different colours to keep the graph easy to read.

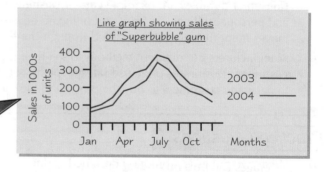

Line graph showing sales of "Superbubble" gum

Sales in 1000s of units

2003
2004

Months

Diagrams can be Misleading

1) Graphs and charts can sometimes give a **false impression** of what is actually going on.

2) If the scales on a graph don't start at **zero**, it can be difficult to see what they show and the meaning can be unclear — e.g. the graph on the right seems to show that the profit has **tripled** between 2004 and 2007, but actually it has only gone up by **10%**.

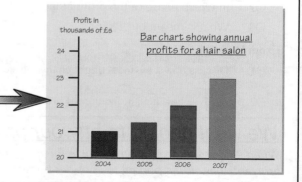

Profit in thousands of £s

Bar chart showing annual profits for a hair salon

Understanding Statistics

You need to be able to *Analyse Data* and *Graphs*

1) As well as being able to read graphs and charts, you need to be able to **analyse** them.
2) This means you need to be able to say what you think is the **important bit** of the chart — e.g. an upward trend in sales, or a big market share.
3) You need to be able to say what you think is **causing** it, and what the potential **effects** might be — e.g. a **decrease** in market share might have been caused by the arrival of a new **competitor**, so the **marketing** budget will have to be **increased** to try to get the market share back.

Data is clustered around an *Average* — *Mean*, *Median* or *Mode*

1) The **mean** is found by **adding together** all the numbers in a data set and **dividing** the total by the **number of values** in the data set. Shops often calculate the mean spend per customer as the starting point of a marketing campaign aimed at increasing customers' spending per shop visit.

> **Example**: 10 customers spend £5.90, £27.98, £13.62, £24.95, £78.81, £16.99, £13.20, £9.95, £2.58 and £14.96.
>
> $$\text{Mean spend} = \frac{5.9 + 27.98 + 13.62 + 24.95 + 78.81 + 16.99 + 13.20 + 9.95 + 2.58 + 14.96}{10} = \frac{208.94}{10} = £20.89$$

2) The **median** is the **middle** value in a data set once all the values are put in **ascending order** — e.g. a business might rank all salespeople by the revenue they've generated over the past month, then identify the **median** and pay everyone above this position a bonus for good performance.

> **Example**: 15 sales people generate revenue of £1200, £1350, £1400, £1500, £1600, £1750, £1900, £1950, £2100, £2200, £2340, £2400, £2450, £2500 and £2950.
>
> **Median sales revenue** = the middle number, which is the 8th number = £1950

3) The **mode** is the **most common number** in a data set. Marks & Spencer might check the modal dress size when planning their shop displays so that the mannequins would reflect the most common body size among British women.

Extensive market research had gone into finding the perfect mannequin to represent today's average British woman.

> **Example**: 15 women have the following dress sizes:
> 10, 12, 16, 14, 12, 14, 8, 18, 16, 14, 12, 14, 10, 14, 16.
>
> **Modal dress size** = 14

Obviously M&S would need a much bigger sample than this.

The *Range* of *Data* is *Important* as well

1) **Range** means the **difference** between the **largest** and the **smallest** in a group of numbers.
2) Averages can be a bit misleading. The **mean** of a **small range** of values is likely to give a **true picture** of the data, but the **mean** of a **large** range of values would give a number somewhere in the middle of the range — this wouldn't show that some of the values were actually really big or really small.
3) A **standard deviation** shows the **spread** of a set of values around the average. You don't have to know how to work out a standard deviation. All you need to know is that a **large** standard deviation means the numbers in the original data set are **spread out**, and a **small** standard deviation means they're **clumped close together**.
4) A **confidence level** is another statistical trick. It indicates how **accurate** a conclusion is likely to be. A confidence level of 95% means managers can assume the prediction would be correct 19 times out of 20.

Understanding Statistics

Businesses work out **Percentage Changes** in figures

1) Businesses work out **percentage** increases or decreases in figures like sales volumes, revenue, profit and market share in order to see how performance is **progressing** over time. By looking at percentage changes over a number of months or years, they can see **trends** in the business' performance.

2) The **formula** for working out percentage change is:

$$\text{Percentage change} = \frac{\text{new figure} - \text{previous figure}}{\text{previous figure}} \times 100\%$$

E.g. if sales of umbrellas have gone up from 9 000 to 11 000, the **percentage increase** in sales is
(11 000 – 9 000) ÷ 9 000 × 100% = 22.2%.

3) It's important not to underestimate large changes in figures even if they only produce a **small** percentage change — e.g. an increase in revenue of £2 million shouldn't be overlooked even if it's only a 3% increase.

Index Numbers show **Changes** in data over time

1) **Index numbers** are a simple way of showing percentage changes in a set of data over time.

2) Businesses take a set of data showing revenue/profits etc. over a number of years, and make the earliest year the **base year** — the value for the base year is set as 100, and the figures for the following years are shown relative to this figure. E.g. the table below shows the index numbers for revenue for an Italian restaurant:

Year	Total Revenue	Revenue Index (2003 = 100)
2003	£17 000	100
2004	£19 550	115
2005	£21 250	125
2006	£22 440	132
2007	£24 650	145

To work out the revenue index for any year, take the total revenue from that year, divide it by the total revenue in the base year and multiply it by 100, e.g. for 2006:

$$\frac{22\,440}{17\,000} \times 100 = 132$$

3) The main **advantage** of indexing is that it makes it easy to see trends within the business.

Businesses **Forecast** what **Future** data will be

1) Businesses use **data** from the **past** to **predict** how the business will perform in the **future** — e.g. if revenue has been going up by around 5% a year for eight years, they might forecast a 5% rise for the coming year.

2) Forecast figures are only **estimates** though — many factors inside and outside the business might influence how it performs, so it's impossible to be certain that the forecast will be accurate.

Practice Questions

Q1 Why can graphs and charts sometimes be misleading?
Q2 Explain the difference between the "mean", "median" and "mode" of a set of data.
Q3 What do index numbers show?

Exam Questions

Q1 Discuss how statistics can hinder as well as help decision-making. (10 marks)

Q2 Explain why statistics are often used in advertising. (9 marks)

There are lies, more lies and statistics...

Statistics can be very helpful but they can also be biased. If you're given a table or graph as part of an exam question, watch out for things like how the axes are labelled, whether the axes start at zero, and whether important info is left out. Remember that businesses often use graphs and charts to put facts and figures in as good a light as possible.

Get Marks in Your Exam

These pages explain how the exams are marked. Basically, the marks are divided up into four different skills — AO1, AO2, AO3 and AO4, and the more skill levels you hit, the more marks you get. Bit like pinball really...

You get marks for **AO1 (showing knowledge)** and **AO2 (applying knowledge)**

AO1 and AO2 questions usually start with words like **"State"**, or **"List"**.

1) **AO1** marks are for **content** and **knowledge**.
2) This means things like knowing the **proper definitions** for **business terms**.
3) You'll only get about 2 marks for AO1, whether the question is a short one worth 2 marks, a shortish one worth 6 marks or a long one worth 15 marks.

> To make sure you'll get marks for content, always give definitions of terms you're using, or formulas if you're doing a calculation.

1) **AO2** marks are for **application** — applying your knowledge to a situation. This means thinking about the **type of business** in the **question**, the product or service it's selling, and the type of market it's in.
2) Numerical **calculations** are also marked as **application**.
3) AO2 is also worth 2-3 marks, but questions which want you to demonstrate AO2 will be expecting you to demonstrate AO1 too, so they'll be worth between 4 and 6 marks overall.

You'll get more marks when you **Analyse (AO3)** and **Evaluate (AO4)**

AO3 marks are for **analysis** — thinking about benefits, drawbacks, causes, effects and limitations.

Analysis questions usually start with words like **"Analyse"**, **"Examine"** or **"Explain why"**.

1) Use your knowledge to **explain** your answer and give **reasons**.
2) If there's data, say what the figures **mean**, talk about what might have **caused** them and say what **effect** you think they will have on the business in the **future**.
3) For top marks, write about **context** — compare a situation with the industry as a whole, or with a competitor.
4) Consider **both sides** of the **argument** — you can only get **limited** analysis **marks** by looking at **one side**.

AO4 marks are for **evaluation** — using your **judgement**.

Evaluation questions usually start with words like **"Evaluate"**, **"Discuss"**, **"Justify"** or **"To what extent"**.

1) **Weigh up** both sides of the argument — consider the **advantages** and **disadvantages** and say which **side** of the argument you think is **strongest**.

2) You don't need a **definite** answer. You can point out that it **depends** on various factors — as long as you say **what the factors are**, and say **why** the right choice depends on those factors. Use your judgement to say what the **most important factors** are. The most important thing is to **justify** why you're saying what you're saying.

It floats — but not on the stockmarket.

3) Relate your answer to the **business described in the question** and to the **situation in the question**. Give reasons why **this business** would make a particular decision, and how and why **these particular circumstances** would affect their decision. For example, there's no point saying that Mr Richards might consider floating his business on the stockmarket if he only has a turnover of £280 000 a year — it's just not a realistic choice for a company of that size.

Get Marks in Your Exam

They give marks for *How You Write*, too

1) You have to use the **right style** of writing and **arrange relevant information clearly** — write a **well-structured essay**, not a list of bullet points. You need to use **specialist vocabulary** when it's appropriate, so it's well worth **learning** some of the **fancy terms** used in this book.

2) You have to write **neatly** enough for the examiner to be able to read it. You also need to use good **spelling**, **grammar** and **punctuation** to make your meaning **crystal clear**. Don't worry, you won't lose marks for spelling errors — but if your handwriting, grammar, spelling and punctuation are **so** far up the spout that the examiner **can't understand** what you've written, **expect problems**.

3) Out of the whole paper, you only get **2** or **3** marks for written communication — but remember that if the examiner can't **read** or **understand** your writing, you won't get the **other marks** either.

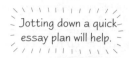
Jotting down a quick essay plan will help.

Dudley got no marks for his "Boston Matrix in Mime".

The Examiner will try to show you *How Much to Write*

1) The examiner does try to help you by telling you how many marks each question is worth and by giving you an idea of how much you need to write.

2) They usually provide about **two lines** for every mark — so for a question worth two marks you'll get four lines.

3) Generally, if the question is worth 2 or 3 marks then you just need to show your business studies knowledge. Give a short answer and move on quite quickly.

4) For a 12 to 15 mark question you need to show analysis and evaluation. You'll have to write much more for these questions. They usually expect you to make a decision, or have an opinion and be able to justify it. There's rarely a right or wrong answer to this sort of question, so just convince the examiner that your opinion is valid by explaining your reasons.

Don't forget to include *All* the *Skills* in *Extended Answer Questions*

When you come up against a long question (worth, say, 15 marks), **don't jump** straight to the **evaluation** stage. The examiner will be looking for **evidence** of the **other skills**, too. So, if they ask you how Mr Frimble can increase his profits, and you think he should either increase his mark-up or make some staff redundant, you need to:

1) **Define** what is meant by mark-up and redundancy (this will get you your **AO1** marks).

2) Explain how mark-up/redundancy are **relevant** to the type of **business/product** that Mr Frimble owns/produces (for **AO2** marks).

3) Give the **advantages** and **disadvantages** of each method of increasing profits (for **AO3** marks).

4) Finally, for the **AO4** marks, **weigh up** both sides of the argument and **decide** if Mr Fimble should increase his mark-up or make some staff redundant (you might decide he needs to do both).

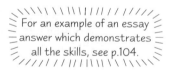
For an example of an essay answer which demonstrates all the skills, see p.104.

It's exam time — let's get down to business...

These pages should take some of the surprise out of your exams. You don't need to know this upside down and back to front like you do the actual business studies stuff. What you do need to know is what the examiners actually want to see from you — not just that you know the facts, but also that you understand and can put to use what you've learnt.

Do Well in Your AQA Exam

*This page is all about how to do well in **AQA** exams. So don't bother reading it if you're not doing **AQA**.*

The **Core Areas** of the specification are divided into **Two Exam Units**

1) **Unit 1** is called **Planning and Financing a Business** — it covers the issues people need to think about when **starting a business**, including **financial planning**.

2) **Unit 2** is called **Managing a Business** — it covers **marketing**, **operations management**, **people in business**, **finance**, and the **competitive environment**. Unit 2 assumes that you know everything that's covered in **Unit 1**, so don't think you can forget all about financial planning etc. as soon as you get out of the first exam.

Unit 1 Exam — 1 hour 15 minutes
1) Based on an unseen case study.
2) Section 1 is usually split up into several **short-answer questions**, worth **2-6 marks** each.
3) Section 2 has several longer **essay-type questions** that ask you to **analyse** or **evaluate** a business decision or method. These are worth **10-15 marks**.
4) There are **60 marks** available, so aim to get a mark about **every minute** — use that as a guide to how long to spend on each question.

Unit 2 Exam — 1 hour 30 minutes
1) **Two unseen case studies**.
2) The first part usually has **one short-answer** question, worth around 4 marks, and then **several longer-answer questions** worth **8-13 marks**.
3) Section 2 has **several short** questions worth **2-6 marks**, and then some **extended-answer questions** worth **8-13 marks**.
4) There are **80 marks** available.

Here's an **Example** of the type of **Case Study** you'll get in the exam

There's a sample question and answer on the next page.

Crinkle Cakes Ltd

Janet Jones had always enjoyed pottering around in her kitchen, and took great pride in the fact that friends and family used to ask her to bake cakes for birthdays and special occasions. However, it was only when one of her friends insisted on paying her £10 for a cake that she first thought of it as a way of making a living.

Eight years on and what had been Janet's sole trader business has grown into a medium-sized private limited company. The business now operates out of premises equipped with machinery which allows them to produce 50 cakes per hour.

The business operates in a very competitive market which is dominated by two national bakeries. It also faces competition from a long-established local firm, which has an excellent reputation in the area. Janet believes that in order to ensure the long-term survival of the business she needs to look at ways in which Crinkle Cakes Ltd could compete more effectively, and achieve its objective of increasing both sales and market share. Money is tight though, since the premises and machinery were obtained using finance which is still being paid off.

Janet had always hoped to see her cakes on the shelves of the big supermarkets, but so far Crinkle Cakes has been unable to secure a deal to supply any of the major chains. The main reasons the supermarkets gave for not stocking Crinkle Cakes products were that they had a very narrow product range (selling only whole cakes rather than multi-pack slices or individual portions), and that their cakes were priced higher than competing bakeries.

Janet and her marketing director Stephen Simms have spent a considerable amount of time looking at ways to address these issues. Stephen did some market research, and he presented Janet with the results (see Appendix 1). Meanwhile, Janet spoke to the operations manager in order to discuss costs. Crinkle Cakes had originally aimed at prices no more than 10% higher than supermarket own-brand prices. The reality though is somewhat different (see Appendix 2). Controlling costs is a real headache due to big fluctuations in the price of raw materials, such as flour. This all gave Janet plenty to think about.

Appendix 1
Results from Market Research (Percentage of People Asked)

Product	Purchased weekly	Purchased monthly	Purchased rarely	Never purchased
Family-sized cake	2	8	62	28
Multi-pack, e.g. slices	55	23	14	8
Individual portions	67	17	10	6

Appendix 2
Recommended Retail Price of Competitors' Products

Company	Family cake	Multi-pack	Individual Portions
Crinkle Cakes Ltd	£5.29	-	-
Local Competitor	£5.09	-	£0.59
National Competitor	£4.49	£1.39	£0.55
Market Leader	£4.99	£1.39	£0.60
Supermarket Own Brand	£3.99	£1.19	£0.49

Do Well in Your AQA Exam

*An **Example Extended Answer** to give you some tips:*

> Suggest a marketing strategy that might ensure that Crinkle Cakes Ltd can continue to compete within their competitive market. (15 marks)

AO1: Refers to, and defines, marketing mix (2 marks)

Any marketing strategy is based around the idea of the marketing mix. This is more commonly referred to as "the four Ps" of product, price, place and promotion. In order to develop a marketing strategy it is necessary to examine each of these four factors in turn.

Stating knowledge is fine, but don't waste too much time

There are a number of factors that need to be examined if Crinkle Cakes wish to improve the product aspect of their marketing. At present they appear to produce mainly family cakes, which 28% of customers never buy according to the research findings in Appendix 1.

Make use of information in the case study

AO2: Links knowledge about marketing mix to business in question (2 marks)

In addition this has meant that few supermarkets have shown a willingness to sell Crinkle Cakes' products. As such I would recommend that they sell a wider range of cake sizes. In addition to the full cakes they could introduce a multi-pack containing cake slices, aimed at families, and single-slice packs, perhaps aimed at single people or impulse purchases. This would widen their target market, since they are likely to be purchased by a different type of consumer. One final alteration that Crinkle Cakes could make to their products is to introduce a range of new cake flavours, though this may require further market research.

AO4: Makes a sensible recommendation after considering evidence (1 mark)

Apply your suggestions to the business in question

Don't waste time repeating the case study, just refer to it

The price that Crinkle Cakes charge for their products is stated in the case study to be higher than their competitors' prices, yet they also indicate that the target price should be no more than 10% above the own-brand products. If they adopt this strategy then the figures given in Appendix 2 show that Crinkle Cakes' prices would be lower than their main three competitors. The strategy should be continued to pursue the objective of increasing sales and market share. However, the study states that the costs of raw materials have prevented this, so steps to control costs would have to be taken to make this possible. Controlling costs is also important while the business is still paying off the cost of its premises and machinery.

It's fine to say you don't think change is needed as long as you explain why

AO2: Links issue of price to business in question (1 mark)

AO3: Considers consequences of financial decisions (1 mark)

AO3: Considers possible risks/problems (2 marks)

As far as place is concerned, Crinkle Cakes must take steps to get their products into the major supermarkets. This should be possible if they make the changes to the product size already discussed.

This is a little vague

The case study does not give any detail about what promotion has taken place. Advertising could be a problem, due to the financial constraints of having to raise finance from within. As such, the company may wish to investigate methods of sales promotion involving tie-ups with other companies. This might be particularly useful if new products are to be launched. The company may also wish to use publicity and public relations to raise brand awareness in a more cost-effective way than advertising.

AO4: Makes a sensible recommendation after considering evidence (1 mark)

Referring to financial restrictions is always a good idea

In conclusion, there are a number of recommendations, as outlined, which Crinkle Cakes Ltd should consider in order to make improvements to their marketing mix, and to achieve the objectives that they have set themselves.

AO4: Makes vague attempt at overall evaluation (1 mark)

Summarising your ideas is a good idea, but make your recommendations clear

This is a reasonably good answer and would get about **11 marks**. It considers a range of marketing options and applies them to the business in the case study. It also makes excellent use of the **information provided** by the examiner. This answer has been set out sensibly with a separate paragraph for each aspect of the marketing mix.

The conclusion is poor and doesn't add anything to the answer. It would've been better if it had made clear which aspects of the marketing mix should be changed as a priority. Remember that the examiner is looking for **evaluation**, and one way of doing this is to explain why it might be better to take one course of action instead of another.

Do Well in Your Edexcel Exam

*This page is all about how to do well in **Edexcel** exams. So don't bother reading it if you're not doing **Edexcel**.*

The AS-level is divided into Two Exam Units

1) **Unit 1** is called **Developing New Business Ideas** — it tests whether you have understood what entrepreneurs need to **do** so that **new business ideas** stand a chance of being **successful** in competitive markets. This includes:

- the **personal characteristics** of successful entrepreneurs,
- **identifying** a business idea that may work,
- **evaluating** a business opportunity (e.g. considering the effects of what's happening in the economy),
- **analysing** or **evaluating** the **finance** needed to set up a business, and planning how to use it.

2) **Unit 2a** is called **Managing the Business** — it covers the **marketing** plan, **budget management**, **managing people** and **managing the provision of goods and services effectively**.

Unit 1 Exam — 1 hour 15 minutes
1) **Section A** is made up of **two-part** questions — the first part is a **multiple-choice** question, and in the second part you have to **explain** why it's the right answer or carry out a **calculation**.
2) You can get a total of **32 marks** for Section A.
3) **Section B** is a **data-response** section — you'll have to show that you **understand** the information and can **analyse** and evaluate it.
4) You can get **38 marks** for Section B.
5) There are **70 marks** available in total, so you should aim to pick up a mark about **every minute**.

Unit 2a Exam — 1 hour 15 minutes
1) This exam has a similar format to the **Unit 1** exam.
2) You can get a total of **24 marks** for Section A.
3) You can get a total of **46 marks** for Section B.
4) There are **70 marks** available in total, so once again you should try to score a mark about once a minute.

Here's an Example Answer to give you some Tips:

This example is based on a case study like the ones in Section B — the real thing would be longer though.

After many years' experience in the general recruitment industry, James Watson and his business partner Ranjit Dalival decided that they wanted to work for themselves.
Before becoming recruitment consultants James had qualified as a mechanical engineer and Ranjit as a chemical engineer. Their current salaries per year, including bonuses, averaged £40 000 each.
They believed that they would be successful if they specialised in the science and engineering recruitment market.

Identify and explain two risks that James and Ranjit are taking in deciding to open their new business. (6 marks)

1 mark (application) — student understands one of the risks.

1 mark (analysis) — uses joint salaries to work out what they need to earn from clients.

1 mark (analysis) — shows understanding of the data research they could do.

In giving up their jobs they would probably hope to earn at least as much as they currently do — £40 000 a year each. They need to be confident that they can get enough business to provide this amount of money and enough to meet their overhead costs such as premises rental and marketing. They need to make sure that sufficient capital has been invested during the start-up period for the company to survive initially.
If the business cannot make a high enough profit to cover the interest on the money that has been invested in it and give enough for re-investment in the business then they may be financially better off working for their current employer.

1 mark (knowledge) — knows meaning of a business term 'overhead costs'.

1 mark (analysis) — understanding that additional data may be needed.

1 mark (evaluation) — given for a correct judgement.

This is a good answer and all the possible marks have been given.
The student has read the question properly and has used a paragraph for each risk.
Analysis and evaluation are clear in the answer and this is what most of the marks are given for.

Do Well in Your OCR Exam

*This page is all about how to do well in **OCR** exams. So don't bother reading it if you're not doing **OCR**.*

The **Core Areas** of the specification are divided into **Two Exam Units**

1) **Unit 1** is called **An Introduction to Business** — it covers the **nature** of business, the **classification** of business, **objectives**, the **market** and other **influences** on business.

2) **Unit 2** is called **Business Functions** — it covers **marketing**, **accounting and finance**, **people in organisations**, and **operations management**. Unit 2 assumes that you know everything that's covered in **Unit 1**, so you'll need to **remember** all those topics too — don't think you can forget all about the nature of business, the market, etc. as soon as you get out of the first exam.

Unit 1 Exam — 1 hour
1) You get **five compulsory questions**, based on an unseen case study.
2) **Part (a)** is usually a short-answer question worth **2-4 marks**, asking you to show your business **knowledge**.
3) **Part (b)** questions are longer essay-type questions worth **10-18 marks** that ask you to **analyse** or **evaluate** a business decision or method.
4) There are **60 marks** available, so aim to achieve a mark **every minute**.

Unit 2 Exam — 2 hours
1) In **Section A** you get **one six-part question** where each part is a **short-answer** question, worth **2-4 marks**
2) **Section B** is based on a **pre-released** case study, so make sure you've **read** it **before** the exam.
3) There are **four** compulsory questions, worth **16-20 marks** each — most of the questions will be longer **essay-type** questions.
4) There are **90 marks** available for this exam.

Here's an **Example Essay** to give you some tips:

> Evaluate the effectiveness of both monetary and non-monetary rewards in motivating staff. (16 marks)

Referring to the theory straight away avoids waffle. (A01: 1 mark)

According to Taylor, people are only motivated by money. If this is true, then a business that pays staff the minimum wage might expect their workers to be demotivated. However, there may be other factors that prevent this from being the case. For example, an employee may be satisfied to work for the minimum wage in the short term since they might think it's better to have a low-paid job (which might lead on to a better job later) than be unemployed. Therefore, the prospects and opportunities that an employee can obtain may also motivate them. Maslow's hierarchy of needs reflects this.

Applies and identifies a possible weakness with the theory (A02: 2 marks)

Refers to a second theory. The answer could get more marks by applying the theory. (A01: 1 mark)

Increasing pay may motivate workers in the short term, particularly in low-paid jobs, but in the longer term it can cause problems. Workers will expect high wages, which may lead to additional problems for a business, since labour costs often make up a large part of a firm's total costs.

It's a good idea to talk about the different effects in the short and long term if you can. (A03: 2 marks)

It's important to look at the effect on the business, not just the workers.

Herzberg believed that two things affect motivation: hygiene factors and motivators. Unless a business provides hygiene factors staff will be dissatisfied, but they will not be motivated simply by these hygiene factors. Therefore, hygiene factors will not motivate staff, but without them the workers will be dissatisfied, even if they have motivators.

Shows knowledge of another motivational theory. Examples of hygiene factors would get more marks. (A01: 1 mark)

Analyses what factors might affect effectiveness of monetary motivation. (A03: 1 mark)

The effectiveness of monetary motivation depends upon current pay rates. Non-monetary rewards are more likely to be effective in businesses where workers are satisfied with their pay. The overall effectiveness of both monetary and non-monetary rewards is therefore dependent upon the individual situation within each business.

Try to write a conclusion that reinforces the key points without repeating bits from your essay. (A04: 2 marks)

This is a **pretty good** answer. It would get about **10 marks**. It uses **business theory** and attempts to **evaluate** the relative usefulness of the two methods of motivation.

It could be **improved** by making the **difference** between the two methods of motivation **clearer**. The **evaluation** could be **developed** by specifying **examples** of where each method might be more useful.

Do Well in Your WJEC Exam

*This page is all about how to do well in **WJEC** exams. So don't bother reading it if you're not doing **WJEC**.*

The AS-level is divided into Two Exam Units

1) Unit 1 (BS1) is called **The Business Framework**. The questions cover topics like:

- **knowing** what different **types** of business enterprise there are, including their **aims** and **objectives**,
- **knowing** what a business' **market** might be and **analysing** how it might be **segmented**,
- **evaluating** how important the different **factors of production** are (e.g. human resources, production methods and business location),
- **analysing** or **evaluating** the **finance** needed for a business, and how to use it.

2) Unit 2 (BS2) is called **Business Functions** — it covers **marketing**, **budget management**, **managing people** and **managing the provision of goods and services effectively**.

Unit 1 Exam — 1 hour 15 minutes
1) This exam is worth **40%** of the AS marks.
2) Each question describes a business **situation** or **problem** and then asks you to show that you **understand** the topic.
3) You have to answer **all** the questions on the paper.
4) Make sure you use **full sentences**, not notes or bullet points.

Unit 2 Exam — 1 hour 45 minutes
1) This exam is worth **60%** of the AS marks.
2) The questions in this section are the **data-response** type.
3) The examiners expect you to do **calculations** and answer questions based on **newspaper articles**.

Here's an Example Answer to give you some Tips:

This example is based on a case study like the ones in BS1 — the real thing would be longer though.

Harry Roberts has taken voluntary redundancy from the steel works he has worked at since leaving school. His redundancy payment was a tax-free £30 000. Rather than look for another job, Harry decided to follow his lifetime ambition of working for himself. He decided to visit a regional franchising exhibition to see what franchises may be available and to question the franchisors exhibiting.

What are the advantages and disadvantages that Harry should consider before going into business as a franchisee? (8 marks)

1 mark (application) — shows advantage of franchising to help make a new business work.

1 mark (analysis) — shows understanding of 'risk'.

1 mark (analysis) — shows understanding of dangers to 'cash flow'.

1 mark (evaluation) — shows a judgement has been made.

1 mark (knowledge) — shows that the student knows the difference between franchisee and franchisor.

1 mark (knowledge) — shows student knows franchises have to be bought.

1 mark (evaluation) — judgement made that it may cancel out why Harry wants to 'go it alone').

Because Harry doesn't have much experience in running a business, signing up to a franchise would be a good idea. The franchisor would train him in sales and finance. He can learn how the business is managed and get advice when he needs it, especially in the first year when most new businesses go bankrupt. Harry would already be selling a proven product or service, which may also already be supported by advertising or promotions.

There are some disadvantages. Harry would have to buy the franchise and make an upfront payment. He would also have to make regular payments to the franchisor. Because franchisors expect their franchisees to set up their business premises in a set way, this can add to the costs of starting up. He would also lose some control over how to run the business.

In my opinion, the disadvantages outweigh the benefits and Harry is likely to decide that owning a franchise is not the best way of working for himself.

This is a **good answer** — it gets **seven marks** for content. The student has **read** the question properly and **referred back** to the case study. As examiners are allowed to give marks for good **spelling** and **grammar**, this answer would get the full **eight**.

Answers to Numerical Questions

Page 31 — Exam Questions
Q2 (a) Maximum of 6 marks available [1 mark for each correct start/finish point of each line]

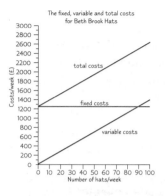

(b) Maximum of 4 marks available.
Costs at 60 hats per week = fixed costs + variable costs **[1 mark]** = 1260 + (60 ×14) = £1260 + £840 = £2100 **[1 mark]** Revenue = selling price × quantity sold = £50 × 60 = £3000 **[1 mark]** Profit = revenue – costs = £3000 – £2100 = £900 **[1 mark]**

Page 33 — Exam Questions
Q2 Maximum of 4 marks available.
Contribution = selling price – variable costs per unit **[1 mark]** Contribution = £13 – £5 = £8 **[1 mark]**
Break-even output = fixed costs ÷ contribution **[1 mark]**
Break-even output = £1000 ÷ 8 = 125 **[1 mark]**

Page 35 — Practice Questions
Q3 Net cash flow = total cash in – total costs
Net cash flow = £8000 – £9500 = (–£1500)
Q4 Closing balance = opening balance + net cash flow
Closing balance = £20 000 + (–£7000) = £13 000

Page 37 — Practice Questions
Q2 Profit budget = income budget – expenditure budget
Expenditure budget = income budget – profit budget
Expenditure budget = £125 000 – £30 000 = £95 000

Page 39 — Practice Questions
Q2 Variance = £15 000 – £18 000 = (£3000)
so there is a £3000 adverse variance

Page 39 — Exam Questions
Q1 Maximum of 8 marks available [1 mark for each of the figures in red entered correctly]

	Feb cumulative variance	Mar budget	Mar actual	Mar variance	Mar cumulative variance
Revenue	£10k (A)	£110k	£120k	£10k (F)	£0
Wages	£9k (F)	£40k	£39k	£1k (F)	£10k (F)
Rent	£1k (A)	£10k	£11k	£1k (A)	£2k (A)
Other costs	£2k (A)	£5k	£5k	£0	£2k (A)
Total costs	£6k (F)	£55k	£55k	£0	£6k (F)

Page 41 — Practice Questions
Q1 Percentage change in profit
= (current profit – previous profit) ÷ previous profit x 100%
Percentage change in profit = (£52 000 – £50 000) ÷ £50 000 x 100 = 4%

Page 41 — Exam Questions
Q1 Maximum of 2 marks available.
ROCE = net profit ÷ capital employed x 100% **[1 mark]**
ROCE = £100 000 ÷ £40 000 x 100% = 250% **[1 mark]**
Q2 (a) Maximum of 4 marks available.
Net profit = gross profit – fixed costs **[1 mark]**

Net profit = £750 000 – £250 000 = £500 000 **[1 mark]** Net profit margin = net profit ÷ revenue x 100% **[1 mark]** Net profit margin = £500 000 ÷ £200 000 x 100% = 25% **[1 mark]**

Page 43 — Exam Question
Q1 Maximum of 4 marks available.
Accounting Rate of Return (ARR) = average annual profit ÷ investment x 100% **[1 mark]**
Average annual profit = £100 000 – £60 000 = £40 000 **[1 mark]** ARR = £40 000 ÷ £200 000 x 100% **[1 mark]**
ARR = 20% **[1 mark]**

Page 51 — Practice Questions
Q2 Absenteeism
= Number of staff days lost ÷ number of working days x100%
Number of working days = 245 x 56 = 13720
Absenteeism = 274 ÷ 13720 x 100% = 1.99%
Absenteeism = 2% (to nearest whole percentage).

Page 63 — Practice Questions
Q1 Capacity utilisation = output ÷ capacity x 100%
42 ÷ 65 x 100% = 65% (to nearest whole percentage).
Q2 Unit cost = total costs ÷ output
£1600 ÷ 450 = £3.56

Page 69 — Exam Questions
Q2 Maximum of 4 marks available

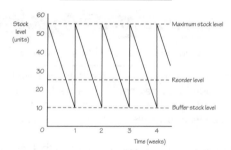

Stock control graph line should start at 550 on the vertical axis **[1 mark]** and finish at 100 **[1 mark]**. The time taken to complete the cycle should be 1 week on the chart **[1 mark]**. The axes should be numbered and labelled correctly **[1 mark]**.

Page 81 — Practice Questions
Q3 Market growth = (new market size – old market size) ÷ old market size × 100% = (£38 million – £33 million) ÷ £33 million × 100% = 15.2% (to 1 decimal place)

Page 81 — Exam Questions
Q2 Maximum of 3 marks available
Market share = sales ÷ total market size × 100% **[1 mark]** Market share = £2m ÷ £19m × 100% **[1 mark]** = 10.5% **[1 mark]**

Page 93 — Exam Questions
Q1 Maximum of 9 marks available.
Sales revenue = price of product x quantity sold **[1 mark]** Sales revenue = £1500 x 200 = £300 000 **[1 mark]** Percentage change in quantity demanded = percentage change in price x elasticity coefficient **[1 mark]** = 15% x 0.7 elasticity coefficient = 10.5% decrease **[1 mark]**. 10.5% of 200 (current sales) = 200 x 10.5 ÷ 100 = 21 **[1 mark]**. New sales = 200 – 21 = 179 **[1 mark]**. New price = £1500 x 115 ÷ 100 = £1725 **[1 mark]**. New revenue = £1725 x 179 = £308 775 **[1 mark]**. Change in revenue = £308 775 – £300 000 = £8775 increase **[1 mark]**.

Index

Index